SAVIOUR'S STORY

J. B. Tucker

PAGE PUBLISHING
Conneaut Lake, PA

First originally published by Page Publishing 2022

ISBN 979-8-88654-440-4 (pbk)
ISBN 979-8-88654-441-1 (digital)

Printed in the United States of America

Joan Tucker
June 2021

*To the tiny orphan who taught us how to live,
love, and smile in spite of life's trials!*

*We wish to thank everyone who helped make this story possible
and ask the reader to understand that the opinions expressed are
those of the authors and include their honest reactions to new
and different cultures. It is in no way meant to pass judgment on
or embarrass but is their best attempt to explain how God works
with all His people regardless of their background, education, or
social status. Our hope is that, through the understanding of our
differences, we can resolve the injustices that permeate our world.*

PREFACE

God made me a mother when I was young and inexperienced. I made many mistakes, and often wish that I could have a "do over." I have apologized to my three beautiful daughters and to our Lord for my poor choices and my egocentric attitude. They have grown up to be incredible women regardless of my faults and failures. Many years later, He decided to give me a second chance.

Let me introduce you to Saviour Nlagnabe, his brothers and sisters and the woman of God who has dedicated her life to them all.

We believe Saviour was born in a mud hut near the village of Gnani in Northern Ghana. In this remote part of the country, many villagers still believe that any birth deformity, natural disaster, or any bad luck befalling the village was the result of evil spirits that can possess a child. These children are condemned to death at the hands of a "concoction man" who is paid by the family to mix poisonous herbs and administer the solution to the child. If the family refuses to kill the child, the entire family is banned from the village and sent to a "witches camp," where water and food are often difficult, if not impossible, to obtain.

Saviour was born with cerebral palsy, and when he was around three years old, it became obvious that he was not going to walk as other babies do and his fate was sealed. His first stroke of "good luck" was that his parents probably did not have the money to hire the concoction man. Instead, he was taken out in the bush and left to the mercy of the wild animals there such as the Black Mamba or worse, to starve to death. Saviour tells us that after three days alone, God sent an angel to rescue him and carry him to the care of Sister Stan Mumuni, who had recently established a home for these precious children.

To counter the stigma of being an evil spirit, she named the orphanage the Nazareth Home for God's Children. When Saviour arrived in 2010, she had taken in a dozen children, four of whom were infants, only a few weeks old. She was the only caregiver, chief cook, and bottle washer, primary fundraiser, and tasked with founding a religious order to care for her children. I called Saviour's abandonment good luck because often the concoction man is unsuccessful; the child would survive but was usually brain damaged. The only recourse is to repoison the child but, in some cases, the child might be handed over to the orphanage. I can only guess at how many of Sister Stan's beautiful children were perfectly normal before the concoction man did his damage.

Nazareth Home relies heavily on individual private donations, so after hiring a few local women to help with the care of these children, she began traveling to Europe and the US to solicit donations for her children. This is where my part of the story comes in.

* * *

It was late August 2014 and my husband and I were just a little over a year into retirement. We thought we kept ourselves busy between yardwork, doting on the grandchildren and church activities. Our pastor was a generous, kindhearted soul who decided to let a relative of his assistant speak to our congregation about the Spirit Children of Northern Ghana and her mission work there. Sister Stan told us the stories of some of the thirty children she had at the orphanage and her efforts to build a self-sustaining community around them to keep them safe and show the people that they were not evil. My heart was so moved by her story and that of her children, I knew I was being called by our Lord to help her.

As a retired nurse, I felt I could be of assistance to her and the children. My husband had a career which had him traveling often, usually with little notice and for undetermined amounts of time. I figured now it was my turn to deploy. He never questioned my decision but supported me as I had supported him. I'd made my plans but they were oh so insignificant to the plans God had for us both.

It took a few months but by February 2015, I had obtained my Ghanaian visa, collected some medical supplies, along with file folders and assessment forms for the children's records. What little room was left in my bags went to a few changes in clothes. I thought I was ready for my two-month mission. Having never traveled overseas alone, I was a bit nervous, especially going to a country so culturally different from my own and a region where mud huts with grass roofs were the norm and the most precious commodity is a glass of potable water.

I purchased a journal in the airport to document my trip, and the cover contained the Scripture verse from Phillipians.4:13, *"I can do everything through Him who gives me strength."* On the first page, at the bottom was Joshua 1:9, *"Be strong and courageous! For the Lord your God is with you wherever you go."* With this affirmation, I knew I was doing what our Lord wanted me to do!

With the help of a new friend who had previously traveled to Ghana, I was met in Accra by a wonderful gentleman, who is an unwavering friend to Sister Stan and all who travel to Ghana to help her. Mr. Emma met me at the airport, helped me get local currency, and gave me a ride to a guest house where he had previously reserved a room for me. He then picked me up the next day after arranging my flight to Tamale, where I would be met by someone from the orphanage for the final leg of the journey.

The combination of what I call travel adrenalin and cautious anticipation meant that I slept fitfully in Accra. After a short flight, I arrived in Tamale, the capital of Ghana's Northern Region. I had been on the road almost forty-eight-hours and was exhausted. Before leaving Tamale, I was told we would be stopping at the hospital to check on one of the children who was suffering from a severe intestinal infection. I would be meeting my first spirit child. Anna was condemned as a "failure to thrive" and rejected by her village. When I first saw her in the hospital, she was three years old and her chart listed her weight as twelve-pounds. I would soon learn that height and weight were not accurate means of estimating age in the orphanage. Many of the children who I thought where infants would turn out to be much older, some in their teens.

We left Anna with her caretaker they called Old Lady after dropping off some food for them as the hospitals do not provide any meals. She would be discharged a few days later with instructions to feed her a paste consisting mostly of ground nuts and fish oil. Anna was a favorite among the other children at the orphanage and would be carried around by various children like a living doll.

As we left Tamale for Sang village, I noticed that even in their larger cities, goats and chickens run free, crossing the roads in front of moving cars. Drivers ED in Ghana seems to consist of how to honk your horn and squeeze your vehicle between seemingly impassable lines of cars, pedestrians, and livestock. As we left the hustle and bustle of Tamale behind us, small villages appeared, growing further and further apart as we journeyed on. Most were just mud huts but all of them would be clustered around the only concrete building in the village, the local Mosque. Children, chickens, sheep, and goats wandered about. Occasionally a "traffic jam" was caused by a herd of cows and the herdsman guiding them to the next water source.

The main road we traveled was dirt, or I should say holes with a little dirt connecting them. Air conditioning in the car is a luxury that is not used as it cuts down on fuel efficiency, so just open the window and enjoy the dust and 100-degree temperatures. Needless to say, the ride was nerve-racking. My driver, Mr. Isaac, apparently knew the location of each pothole and would artfully swerve from one side of the road to the other to avoid them. Oncoming traffic would honk their horn (Ghanaian for "Get back in your lane, I'm coming through"). Combine this with the pedestrians, livestock, and complete absence of a speed limit and I must say, tired as I was, I was very much awake when we reached the orphanage. Turning down the lane that led to the orphanage main gate, the adrenalin from the ride subsided, and I realized I was tired, hungry and feeling a little sorry for myself.

All of that disappeared as we entered Nazareth Home. I was greeted by dozens of smiling faces, singing "You are welcomed in the name of the Lord…" They brought me to tears! Such beautiful, precious children. They all wanted to hug me or have me carry them. They already called me Mama Joan. I would later find out that it is customary for younger ladies to be called Auntie while us seniors are addressed as Mama. After a welcome dance in the dining hall, I was fed a local meal of ground nut soup served with a lump of uncooked pasty bread made of corn meal called banku. You tear some banku off and dip it in the soup before eating it. No utensils required. In fact, most meals are eaten using your God-given utensils we call fingers. Thankfully, Sister realizes that foreign visitors have different preferences so I usually found a knife, fork, and spoon awaiting when I sat down.

The orphanage sits in a compound with the main building laid out like a large letter "E". My room was next to Sister's in the center of the building surrounded by the children. It was here that I got to experience my first of many bucket baths. Water is very scarce and I would find out that running water is even scarcer. A shower consisted of ladling water from a large bucket kept in your bathroom over yourself, lathering up and repeat to rinse. The water was at room temperature which, in Ghana I figured meant around 100 degrees. Not even close. What at first was shockingly cold became refreshingly cool and the lack of hot water became a minor inconvenience after a few days. In fact, after a hot day on the dusty road, it was rather refreshing.

I was restless that first night in spite of my fatigue. Besides the new surroundings, new experiences, and me trying to imagine what might be next, every night I heard sounds of babies crying, a rooster who had no concept of dawn, and the friendly neighborhood Iman's call to prayer at 11:00 p.m. and 4:00 a.m. in the village next to the orphanage.

* * *

The next morning, I was up early and got my first look at what life was like at Nazareth Home for God's Children. The children sleep five or six in a room with a room mother or Auntie who is responsible for them. The day starts with a bucket bath, then it's off to breakfast at the dining hall. A bath for them is an outdoor operation and pretty much follows the same wet, lather, and rinse routine although their bucket of water would be mixed with some warmed on the fire. They are dressed in uniform shirts and pants for boys or dresses for the girls. After grace and breakfast, some of the children are off to classes while others go into the yard to play.

There were thirty-two children at the orphanage on my first visit. Some appeared to have minimal, if any, disability. I was told that most of these children were sent here due to the death of their mother during birth or, if they were twins, two more reasons for being labeled a spirit child. Other reasons can be causing a drought or famine, death of a family member or villager, seizures, outbreak of cholera, or typhoid fever, and the list goes on and on. One child was sent because someone in his village said he appeared to them in a dream, and he threatened her.

In the days that followed, I would clean and bandage many wounds—cuts, abrasions, insect bites—treat rashes, fevers, and upset stomachs. I took numerous children to the Tamale Teaching Hospital and to Tamale West Hospital, over an hour drive from Nazareth Home, to be seen and treated by specialists. Most of them were suffering from seizure disorders and needed daily medicine to control their "falling." Others suffered from malaria or gastroenteritis. Occasionally, we would take a child to the Yendi Hospital which was closer (around forty-five minutes from Sang Village) but much smaller than the Tamale hospitals.

My introduction to health care in Northern Ghana was another eye opener. The hospitals were crowded and not up to Western hygiene standards. Besides the scarcity of water, the absence of air conditioning allows the Harmattan winds to blow through open windows and doors, coating every surface with a film of dirt and sand. The Harmattan is a dry, dusty wind that blows in from the Sahara through Ghana from December to March every year.

On one of my first visits, I was trying to wash my hands after changing a dirty diaper only to be told by one hospital employee, "Mama, just because there are sinks doesn't mean there is water!" I was directed to a large plastic can containing water in the corner of the room.

My biggest shock, however, was when I was told one of the children needed IV fluids. I was given a prescription and pointed to the nearest pharmacy where I could purchase the saline solution needed for the IV. This is the same procedure if you need a shot, bandage, or stitches. The family is responsible for purchasing any medication, IV fluids, bandages, and bringing them to the hospital to be used on the patient. They also have to provide meals for the patient and their caretaker who is required stay with the patient at all times.

One of the children who seemed to be in the greatest need of medical attention was Abraham. Abraham has hydrocephalus, or water in the brain. His tiny four-year-old body could barely support the weight of his growing head. He always looked sad and in pain. Children with hydrocephalus are unable to allow the fluid produced in the brain to empty out by absorption through the spinal cord. The obstruction causes increased pressure which pushes the brain into the skull. Without intervention, it begins to destroy the brain tissue. The corrective surgery installs a shunt in the brain that bypasses the blockage and allows the fluids to be absorbed in the abdomen. It is a procedure that needs to be repeated to lengthen the shunt as the patient grows and is fraught with potential complications such as infection or blockage in the shunt.

I was dreading the thought of this child being hospitalized in these circumstances and felt it would be best if I could get him to the United States for treatment. In fact, Sister Stan had already purchased two shunts, one for a little girl named Mary. Unfortunately, she died when her shunt became infected, so Sister decided not to risk Abraham suffering the same fate. If nothing else, this made me more determined to find a way to save this little boy.

A few weeks later, the reality of how harsh life can be here was brought home when Baby Anna died. She had been in and out of the hospitals in Tamale and Yendi but had regressed and been rushed to the closer Yendi hospital for emergency treatment. Unfortunately, she was too far gone, and at five thirty one morning, she passed away. A driver was sent to retrieve her body and bring back Old Lady who had been with her. Her body was laid in the chapel where the women bathed and clothed her in a white dress. The local carpenter was called and made a simple wooden box for a coffin. A small group of us accompanied her and Father Isadore to an area Sister has had to use too many times to bury one of her children. It was just before noon that same day that Anna was laid to rest. My first spirit child was safe with the Lord.

My plans to remain were interrupted when I was called home a few weeks early to the bedside of my mom who had suffered a stroke. I spent some time with her in a rehabilitation hospital and then headed home to explain my plans for Abraham to my husband.

* * *

After I returned home, I was determined to find a way to help Abraham. Children suffering from physical disabilities like hydrocephalus have little hope for a productive future. Left untreated, in addition to pain and suffering, infant hydrocephalus leads to significant brain damage, severe developmental delay, blindness, and ultimately death. With the help of some friends, I made contact with a neurosurgeon at the Medical University of South Carolina (MUSC). He told me that, while MUSC does surgery to correct hydrocephalus, they would not be able to assist with this child because there was a hospital that specializes in this condition in Africa. He gave me the information I needed to get in touch with the CURE Hospital outside of Kampala, Uganda. It seems my travels to help the spirit children of Ghana would soon have me heading from West to East Africa.

It took some doing, but by January 2016, I had finalized plans with the director of CURE Hospital Uganda. From their website, I found that *"CURE Uganda is recognized as a global leader in a minimally-invasive, shuntless treatment for hydrocephalus. Developed by the hospital's founding medical director, Dr. Benjamin Warf, this procedure combines endoscopic third ventriculostomy (ETV) with a choroid plexus cauterization (CPC) to provide a safer, more sustainable solution than the use of a shunt."*

I watched my husband's eyes glaze over reading the text, so I explained that they would microscopically burrow from the top of

Abraham's skull to the brain stem. They would then create an opening that would allow the fluids to drain into the spinal column and then be absorbed. The benefit to this procedure is that, if successful, the opening grows with the patient and no further surgeries are ever required and the possibility of infection is near zero. The cost per patient was $1,000.00 regardless of the length of stay or any extra services provided (a policy which proved a God-send for us.) A wonderful and loving family member donated the cost of hospitalization and surgery, and with the generosity of many others, we were able to cover the airfare for Abraham, Sister Stan, and myself.

This is when I had my first taste of bureaucracy at work. Visas in Africa can take a long time and often require multiple trips to the embassy in Accra. It is also required that the person applying for the visa must do so in person. This meant that Sister Stan would have to travel there with Abraham to apply. So Sister Stan would have to drive an hour or so to the nearest airport, take the flight to Accra, deal with the embassy and, if lucky, make it back to the airport in time to fly back home before the airport there shuts down for the evening (no runway lights.) Airfare alone would cost the orphanage $400.00. She could take Abraham by bus to Accra which was less expensive but would mean a total of twenty-four hours on the road each trip. It took a while but by early February, the visas were approved, and we were able to purchase our airline tickets for February 7. We were scheduled to arrive at the hospital by Monday, February 8, with surgery the next day and discharge the following Tuesday.

We would be leaving the orphanage early in the morning on February 6 by truck for a six-hour drive to Kumasi, according to Google maps, where we would spend the night. Then it would be just a four-hour drive to Accra to catch our flight the next day. That was the plan but as the saying goes, "If you want to hear God laugh, tell Him your plans." Our early morning departure was delayed by a group of Muslim men who came unannounced to see Sister and the children. They heard about Sister's devotion to these abandoned children and wanted to witness this for themselves. They brought a truck full of gifts for the orphanage to include diapers, crackers, rice, juice, and much more! They were all holding the babies and were amazed at all she had accomplished in just a few years. They thanked her profusely for caring so much; it was a very touching moment.

Finally, around 3:00 p.m., we were loaded up in the Tundra truck and ready to go. Patience was never my strong suit, and I just had my first lesson in "African time." Sister loved to remind me that we were not in America! Our driver, Mr. Alahassan, was wonderful and very patient with me but had never looked at Google maps. The trip took more like eight hours with us arriving around 11:00 p.m. We were settled into the guest quarters of the local rectory for the night. The next morning, we attended 6:00 a.m. Mass in the parish church, which was undergoing renovations. It had open ceiling beams and no roof, but it was beautiful! We had a most joyous celebration with a full choir and keyboard accompaniment. All the parishioners were dressed in beautiful African clothing. Mass was said in the local dialect, but Father gave a special mini homily for me in English. It was a very touching service.

We were back on the road at 11:00 a.m. headed to Accra International. Again, Google maps didn't account for actual road conditions, and we arrived at 7:00 p.m. We made a mad dash to the counter, got our baggage checked, document shot records checked, and filled out immigration forms. They were calling for all passengers on our flight to come immediately so, of course, I was delayed by security who confiscated my hemostats (a surgical tool that looks like scissors but can clamp and hold firmly) and scrutinized my Fitbit as if it were some sort of alien weapon. We hurried to the gate and finally got to our seats in time for the nine thirty flight.

All this time, poor Abraham was going into panic overload. He had never before experienced an escalator, riding in a transport bus, or boarding an airplane. He kept repeating, "I do not want to enter" and required coaxing for each new obstacle that blocked his path. Once seated, we were served dinner, but Abraham was so exhausted he fell asleep and did not eat. We stopped for a flight change in Kenya with a two-hour layover. We had a very long walk from gate four to gate twenty-three so the layover was a blessing in disguise.

This leg of the flight took only one hour, and we were finally in Uganda. Nothing could go wrong now.

* * *

After landing in Entebbe International Airport, we were greeted by a taxi driver prearranged by the hospital. This was not to be the fifteen- or twenty-minute cab rides we are used to in the States. We ran into very heavy traffic and the trip to the hospital in Mbale took us seven hours! All the time Abraham appeared very lethargic and feverish, and then he began vomiting. We arrived at the hospital around 7:00 p.m. where he was checked by a nurse, and we were escorted to the private room, which cost $20 per day, meals included. That night was not a very restful one as Abraham's condition did not improve and the nurses came in every few hours for vital signs.

The next morning, the doctor came into examine him. And ordered a CAT scan and blood work. Around three thirty that afternoon, we were given the news that the fever and vomiting was due to Abraham having severe malaria. The parasite destroys red blood cells and Abraham's had a hemoglobin of 6.0 g/dl. Normal for children his age is from 11–15g/dl. He needed IV fluids, anti-malaria drugs, and a blood transfusion. They could not operate on him until he is at least 9 g/dl.

His CAT scan showed how much his brain was being compressed by the fluid and pressure. Normal brain scans show all the ridges and valleys—medical names are gyri and sulci—that cover our cerebrum. In Abrahams initial scan, his brain was smooth as a rock, meaning he had very high pressures. The multiple blood draws and IV insertion caused poor Abraham great anxiety, and his way of expressing his displeasure was to cry, "Why? Why?" It broke my heart to hear this, and I could only snuggle him in my arms and try to comfort him during these difficult times.

Three days later after receiving IV meds, and two units of blood, Abraham was finally well enough to go to surgery. The doctor came in to tell us when he would go to the operating room. Abraham heard him say we could go tomorrow and thought that meant he was going home. He grabbed his backpack and started shoving his toy animal, Dog, and his belongings into the sack. Of course, he was not too thrilled to learn what the doctor really meant. His surgery on February 9, my plan, was scheduled for the next morning, Friday, February 12. On the day of surgery, his head was shaved, and he was given some sedation.

Before he was taken to the operating room, the nurses asked if they could pray over Abraham. We joined hands and prayed that God would guide the surgeons and nurses and protect him during the procedure. I was then allowed to carry him to the operating suites. The surgical nurse took the sleeping child from my arms and walked through the doors to the sterile area where the neurosurgeons awaited.

Sister and I waited and prayed for a successful surgery. If they were unable to complete the final step, he would be given a shunt. Around two thirty that afternoon, we were informed that he was in recovery and expected to arrive in the Intensive Care Unit (ICU) within thirty minutes. We went to the ICU when summoned by the staff. He was wide awake and asking for something to eat! We gave him some biscuits and sips of water. He took these then begged for rice! We were permitted to give him a small amount, and he devoured it.

Typically, the child stays in ICU overnight and the caregiver is permitted to get some rest in their room; typically. Around eleven that night, I was called to the unit by a nurse telling me "Abraham is calling for you." I rushed to the room to find four nurses around his bed and a naked, crying child, standing up, calling, "Mama Joan! Mama Joan!" As I went to hug him, he sobbed, "Mama Joan, I need to urinate!" I guess it never dawned on him that the nurses would be able to help him. Abraham and I bonded, and he didn't want me out of his sight. So I dozed off in the chair next to his bed for the remainder of the night. So much for a restful night.

Sister was staying in a convent near the hospital and had the opportunity for daily Mass, and she would bring me communion each day. She arrived around 8:30 a.m. to relieve me and allowed me to get some rest. Abraham returned to our room Saturday afternoon and things seemed to go back to what for us was considered normal. The doctors came in to explain to Sister and I that the operation had some glitches.

During this procedure, they usually cauterize the part of the brain that produces the fluid. Then they microscopically proceed to near the brain stem where they form a single conduit into the spinal cord for drainage. It seems that Abrahams condition was what they called Post Infectious Hydrocephalus. They believe that when he was forming in his mother's womb, she must have had an infection and that this caused a web of scars to form around his brain stem and block the release of the fluid. Because of the extensive scarring, instead of forming one large opening, they formed three small openings. He still had a chance for a successful outcome, but we wouldn't know for about one year. The doctor said that if he is still draining after a year, he should be good for the rest of his life. It's all in God's hands now!

* * *

On Monday, February 15, we were finally given the clearance to leave. We had airline tickets for the following day but were warned that there was an election coming up on Wednesday and that there could be civil unrest here if it doesn't go as the people want.

We left the hospital around two o'clock that afternoon and were taken to an inn suggested by the driver. We did stop for a visit at the home of the driver's family, and he gave us the scenic tour of Uganda. What a very lush country compared to Ghana. Crossing the Nile was a beautiful sight and Sister saw a gorilla in the bush on the side of the road. I missed it as I was watching Abraham sleep and asking God to make this good for him. Dinner was on the road, and we arrived at the inn at 10:00 p.m. Overnight accommodations were beautiful but very hot. The inn keeper obligingly got us a fan which made things more comfortable, and we had running water but there was no hot water. Life was good.

The next morning, we were treated to a traditional, British-style breakfast, complete with tomatoes, beans, hard boiled eggs, toast, and potatoes. We boarded Rwanda Air at 11:30 a.m. for our 12:00 p.m. flight. The return flights were uneventful with stops in Rwanda and Nigeria and finally home to Ghana.

Sister had made arrangements for us to stay at a guest house in Accra, operated by Catholic priests. It was very nice and most comfortable. We had a great night's sleep and were awakened at six thirty for breakfast. Then we headed back to the airport for the local flight to Tamale. Abraham and I were going to fly while Sister Stan and Mr. Alahassan would drive the truck home, making stops on the way to purchase fresh fruits and vegetables that are very difficult to buy in the Northern Region. Abraham was tearful when they dropped us off. I am sure he would be very happy to never board an airplane again! The flight was uneventful, and we arrived at Nazareth Home again to be greeted by joyful, singing children. They were so happy to see Abraham, and he was also glad to see them, especially Chumba a.k.a. Lucy. They were very close to each other.

So my planned trip of six days had taken just a little over ten. I chalked part of this off to "Africa time," but I know for certain that God had a one extra thing in mind that would take a little longer than my plan allowed. While we were waiting for Abraham to heal so he could have his surgery, I asked the taxi driver to take me to the market area to buy dinner for us. While shopping, I saw a disabled gentleman with flip flops on his hands, dragging himself across the busy streets in an attempt to beg for money or food. This took my breath away. He reminded me so much of a little boy at the orphanage, Saviour, who had lower leg deformity cause by cerebral palsy and would drag himself around using his hands.

I remember him crawling into a shallow concrete channel used to direct rainwater away from the buildings and towards an area that would be used for vegetable gardening. There he would wedge his legs into the opening and use the concrete to support himself into a pretend standing position. Then he would wave frantically at me and use that million-dollar smile to get my attention. When I'd ask him if he wanted to stand, his grin would just get bigger, and he would nod his head yes. I knew in my heart that Saviour deserved so much more in his life than flip flops and begging. It was at that moment the Holy Spirit told me I needed to help him next.

For the next week, things returned to what I called orphanage normal. I put many plasters (band aids) on wounds and treated the children with ringworm. Some of the children were having frequent seizures and two others were running fevers and vomiting. We took these two to the Yendi Hospital where one was treated for malaria and the other admitted for pneumonia and sepsis. Sepsis is the body's extreme response to infection that can damage healthy cells causing organ failure, shock, and even death.

Sister requested I take four of the children to be checked by the neurologist at the Tamale Teaching Hospital because of their repeated seizures. We left early in the morning, getting there around 8:00 a.m. It took two hours to obtain the medical records from the front receiving area, pay the usual fee, and find our way to the neurology clinic. Upon arriving I was told that because it was a specialty clinic, I needed to go back to the front cashier and pay fifty cedi—about ten dollars—more for each child. Back in line for another hour.

A Ghanaian queue or line is more a suggestion and in no way resembles an orderly line of people waiting their turn. Much like their driving habits, standing in a queue meant finding the smallest opening in the crowd to push ahead. So a frustrating hour later, fully loaded with all the paperwork and receipts, I headed back down the hallway with the children. We sat in the crowded hallway for half an hour when a nurse came to the door and announced that the doctor would not be coming until the end of the month. I had to use every ounce of self-control not to unleash the "Ugly American" that had been brewing inside for the past few hours. I couldn't afford to alienate these people that I knew would be seeing these children on a regular basis. I was obviously an outsider but I was representing the Nazareth Home for God's Children so I tempered my response; with His help.

I was able to stop in Tamale to purchase my airline ticket back to Accra and was able to get a flight leaving Tamale at 1:30 p.m. on Thursday, February 25. I was already booked on a flight to Charleston through Atlanta that evening leaving at 11:30 p.m., so the timing couldn't be better. That should have worried me.

The night before a guests' departure becomes an occasion to celebrate their visit. Special meals are prepared for all, usually with meat included in the main dish as an added bonus. The children love the food, singing, and dancing. They usually present a heartfelt thank you message to the visitor often written and read out loud by one of the older children. These meals create a precious forever memory for me. I do love these children and will keep them in my heart and prayers forever! Each and every one of them has the light of Christ in their eyes! I was able to see the children the next morning at breakfast to say my goodbyes. There were many tears, mine and theirs, especially Abraham's. I promised them I would be back and gave kisses and hugs to all.

* * *

We left for the Tamale airport arriving by 12:30 p.m., plenty of time to check in and get my seating assigned. We were met at the entrance by a flight attendant telling us that all flights have been grounded. The Harmattan winds had raised too much dust making visibility too poor for safe flying. No problem though, they would reevaluate again tomorrow morning. I was dumbfounded. Now what do I do? I am scheduled to leave Accra at eleven thirty this evening! Choking back the tears, I called Sister for advice. Luckily, I had purchased my airfare from a company that specializes in missionary fares, and I was able to change my flight to the following day for a minimal fee. I did not want to chance the Harmattan shutting down the airport again tomorrow so, after checking around with the locals, I found that the most reliable way to Accra was on the overnight bus. The fare was half the cost of airfare but took ten times longer.

So I booked a seat on the 5:00 p.m. bus. I hurried to purchase a dinner from a local restaurant and was transported to the bus terminal. When I arrived, I saw how close the seats were to the row in front of them. Less leg room than the average economy flight. I did notice the seat in the very back of the bus was a bench seat and the center was not occupied. Lots of leg room there. I hurriedly sat down congratulating myself on choosing this coveted seat, until we actually began the trip. I soon found out I was directly over the engine compartment and the floor became so hot I swear that at one point it was glowing. I am sure the locals laughed to themselves over the dumb American. Anyway, before I realized the folly of my choice, we waited, and waited, and waited. I was being introduced to another Ghanaian tradition.

It seems a 5:00 p.m. departure time was contingent on having a full bus. With so many customers on Africa time, it was 7:30 p.m. before the doors were closed and the driver pulled out of the lot. I had consumed my chicken and rice dinner and looked for a place to discard my trash. I saw no trash bins, so I hung onto it until our first stop. Surely there would be some stops for stretching and bathroom breaks.

The floor became burning hot after about thirty minutes, so I had to put my carry-on bag on my lap with the refuse from my dinner. I did have a bottle of water with me, which I consumed quickly due to the heat. I tried to doze off but, unfortunately, this bus included entertainment in the form of a Ghanaian soap opera being shown on a large central screen with the dialogue blaring from the intercom system making sleep an impossibility. You see, the general theme of these soap operas involves very little acting and a lot of screaming; usually just as I was dozing off.

Finally, the bus pulled to a stop after a few hours. I looked around and saw nothing but darkness out there! Not a rest stop, gas station, market…nothing. So the bathroom break consisted of stepping over all the trash thrown into the center aisle, and exiting the bus to squat on the dirt to relieve yourself. I needed to go so badly, so "when in Rome…" It was not an easy task for an older woman. My core strength was minimal, but I refused to put my hands on the ground to balance myself or to stand up! Needless to say, I survived and I think with a little practice, I'll be able to avoid hitting my sandals next time.

We arrived in Accra at 5:00 a.m. and my friend and guardian angel, Mr. Emma, came for me and my luggage. He took me to the

Baptist Guest House to sleep for a few hours and would return for me later. I had to be at the airport early to finalize my new itinerary and get new tickets. At this point, I'm twelve hours behind my planned schedule but I'm at the international airport and should be home soon. I know they recommend you arrive early for international flights but I think I broke the record. My stay at the airport in Accra was a little over ten hours as my much-delayed flight departed at eleven thirty that evening.

Because of the last-minute change in departure, courtesy of the Harmattan, a flight to New York or Atlanta was not possible. My only option was to be rerouted through Detroit Michigan. When I arrived there, I had been traveling for fifty-nine hours and was I very discouraged. I was also getting very tired, and I found the combination of the two made me very chatty. A nice older gentleman sat down next to me as we waited for our flight to Atlanta. He was carrying a book about Africa so I proceeded to tell him all about Sister Stan and her children. He listened politely and probably wondered why he always sits next to the chatty ones.

What I didn't know at the time was I really wasn't talking to him. A young lady sitting behind me leaned over her seat and said, "I hope you don't mind me eavesdropping, but my name is Hallie Lord and I am hosting a session on the Catholic Radio Station. I would love to have you come on the show and tell our audience about Sister Stan and her children." It was at that moment I knew my delays were not an inconvenience, but an opportunity sent by God to help me spread the message about the orphanage.

All I could think about was "Thank you, Lord!" This would be yet another "God moment," one of many to come in the next few years. All I would have to do is come back to Detroit to be on Hallie's show. As it turns out, Hallie was heading home herself and surprise, we live just a few miles from each other. It took the Harmattan winds, a cancelled flight, the bus ride I'd sooner forget, and rerouting seven hundred miles out of my way to Detroit for us to meet. I won't even mention the patient gentleman with a book on Africa or our choosing back-to-back seats. That's all just a big coincidence, right?

I made arrangements to meet Hallie the following Friday at her home/radio studio. The day arrived, and I nervously put on my headset and, after some preliminary instructions, started the show. To tell you the truth, the next few minutes were a complete blur to me, but at the end of the interview, Hallie asked me what would help me with my next trip to Ghana. I told her that I was able to do some basic evaluations on the children, but I had minimal experience with physical therapy. Many of the children suffered from illnesses or injuries that limited their ability to perform functional activities and they would benefit greatly from that sort of expertise.

If you think getting me seven hundred miles out of my way to meet Hallie was something, how about three thousand? It turns out that just outside Los Angeles, California, a Physical Therapist named Marie was driving to work and, while she missed a lot of the broadcast, she heard that last part and decided she had to help. She called the radio station and eventually, they got us connected. After a lot of phone calls, we finally met at JFK airport the following year on our way to Ghana. She has made the trip three or four times since and been an incredible help to the children. I can honestly say that without her help and expertise, I would not be writing Saviour's story right now. I owe her a great deal and am very proud to call her my friend.

* * *

Gnani Village, Northern Ghana
20 December, 2010
Application for the acceptance of rejected child.
Child's name: Saviour Mbamba

Dear MASEL,

Greetings of peace and joy in the Holy Spirit from the Good Shepherd rectorate, Gnani. It is the will of God that all should be saved and have life to the fullest. This is why Christ came to dwell among us.

By this letter, I want you to accept a rejected child who is so dear to my heart. I got this child in one of my outstations and want you to help me save the life of this child.

I hope this letter will meet your kind consideration. May the Good Lord, Jesus Christ, and God the Father in oneness with the Holy Spirit bless you and your ministry,

Yours in Christ,
Fr. Peter Jabaab

With this letter from a parish priest in Northern Ghana, Saviour began his journey that would ultimately take him thousands of miles from the village that had rejected him. Sister Stan accepts all the children presented to her and is committed to giving them the fullest life filled with dignity and love for as long as they live. I was determined to take it one step further for Saviour.

Once back in the United States, Bill and I began our search for the answer to my latest calling. Eventually, I got in touch with Shriners Hospital in Greenville, South Carolina. This hospital specialized in treating patients with cerebral palsy, in particular those with lower limb deformities. They also welcomed and cared for international children. The perfect solution was just a few hours away from where we lived. One more of many God moments we would have in the coming months and years. Now all I had to do was get back to the orphanage and do the preliminary examination on Saviour for the doctor. I knew that, with Marie's help, we would give him the best evaluation possible.

Either I'm the worlds unluckiest traveler or there is never a good time to travel to Africa. I met up with Marie in New York in January where our flight was immediately delayed over two hours while we waited for our plane to be deiced. This, of course, got us into Accra just in time to miss the last flight to Tamale so back to the Baptist Guest House in Accra for the night. We got a flight out just after midday, so with the hour and a half drive to the orphanage from Tamale, we should be there in time to unpack and see the children before supper.

As we waited for our luggage, a flight attendant came to us and explained that our luggage had been left in Accra due to weight concerns (forget the $40.00 overweight charges we'd paid.) But not to worry, the luggage would definitely be on the last flight of the day at 4:00 p.m. (Africa time!) Rather than wait at the airport, Mr. Alahassan drove us into Tamale to visit the children from the orphanage who were attending a private school there. These are a few children who have the ability and potential to learn. Sister has private sponsors, mostly from the US, who make a monthly donation to pay for the child's tuition, room, and board.

Amazingly, the luggage did arrive but our midafternoon arrival time at the orphanage became a just after dark arrival. This did not dampen the spirits of the children who greeted us with song and dance and a special gift of plastic flowers (growing real ones is a waste of precious water) from my buddy Abraham and his friend, Blessing. Dinner followed this welcoming ceremony, and we were finally able to get to bed around ten thirty that night. Saint Christopher, guardian of travelers, can you spend some time with the airlines please?

I think it might be best to explain the evolution of Saviour's name at this point. When I first met him, his name was Xavier. To this day, I'm not sure if this was a typo on the Ghanaian health card or the Ghanian/Brit accent that can challenged the untrained Yankee ear at times. It was only when I saw his passport a year or so later that I saw his first name was Saviour. In addition, his last name was listed as Mumuni, Sister Stan's last name. This would later morph into a last name of Mbamba and would only change one last time when his passport also told us that Mbamba was his middle name and Nlagnabe was his official last name. It seems that names in Ghana are like time tables and posted schedules; more a suggestion than a hard fact. Birthdates apparently are also negotiable as he had two; one in 2005, the other in 2007. The folks at the passport office chose the latter. My apologies to friends and family for the confusion and specially to Shriner's Hospital for the additional paperwork and time it took to turn Xavier Mumuni into Saviour Mbamba Nlagnabe in all your records.

The next few weeks were filled with happy children, occasional sibling squabbles and a lot of evaluations and therapy for the most physically challenged. Saviour, of course, was our main focus. Marie's training and expertise were crucial in getting an in-depth evaluation of Saviour's abilities and limitations for the doctor at Shriners to base his decision on whether to take him as a patient.

By January 15, 2017, Marie and I had finished our evaluation, and I nervously emailed our findings to Dr. Westbury at Shriners for his consideration. This included Maries notes and some photos we'd taken showing Saviour's condition. We made arrangements to have x-rays taken, but I was impatient and wanted to get the ball rolling. I was slipping into the "my time, my schedule" mode, forgetting that He knows so much better than I. In order to distract me, Sister Stan gave Marie and I such a beautiful gift. On January 22, we would become the godmothers to two beautiful baby girls who had recently arrived at Nazareth Home. We were both so honored to stand in witness as Fr. Isadore baptized Joanna and Noella, and we welcomed them into the community of faith.

It would be almost ten days more, and several impatient emails to Lisa at Shriners before we would hear from the doctor. He wanted us to send a hard copy of the X-rays and a video of Xavier walking. I explained that he cannot walk or even stand without help, but I sent it anyway. Later that day, I received the decision from the doctor. It stated that "Xavier was beyond the scope of what we can treat in Greenville for an international patient" and that he, regretfully, could not accept him as a patient.

* * *

While this was a terrible blow for us, Dr. Westbury didn't just say no, but spent the time to find an alternative for us to consider.

He said that there was a hospital in Ghana that might see him. I was told it was an orthopedic hospital in Accra called FOCOS Hospital. I prayed that this would be as good for Saviour as the CURE Hospital had been for Abraham. We could not get an appointment before February 17, which meant another change of airline ticket home. In what was becoming routine for me, the day we left the orphanage; the truck broke down, and we were too late for our flight to Accra. So we were back on the overnight bus! This bus, however, was the VIP bus, much roomier than the first and actually had working air conditioning. It did however play the same six hours of Ghanaian soap operas, with all the screaming, shouting, and hokey music!

Saviour, Mr. Alhassan, and I arrived at the FOCOS hospital in time for the 10:30 appointment. After the doctor's visit and exam, he seemed hopeful that Saviour could be helped. He explained what procedures he intended to do and stated that he would then be placed in a fully body cast from "nipples to toes" with a bar between his knees. He would only have to remain in the cast for six weeks! FOCOS is a private hospital and, as such, were not obligated to accept all patients presented. They told me they would send me the decision by email along with the cost estimate for the procedure. I left from there feeling a bit more hopeful as it seemed the doctor saw the possibilities that I did with this boy. Caring for a ten-year-old in a full body cast for six weeks was a daunting challenge but I had to trust in the Lord.

On March 2, 2017, I received the estimate from the hospital and it quickly became clear this was not going to be like our experience with Abraham. The estimate was broken into two pages, one for each leg, although the procedures would be done on the same day. The combined cost was 53,550 cedi total! At the current rate of 3.8 cedi per US dollar, it was going to cost $14,000! At the time I was so focused on the cost of the operation, it didn't dawn on me until much later that post-operative visits, physical therapy (if available), and the special equipment he would need could easily double that amount.

My husband and I started fund raising using social media and got such an incredible response to our plea to "Help Xavier walk" from family and friends and people we'd never met. Within a few weeks, we had raised half of the total needed. I knew that the generosity of the people in this country would not let us down and, while this eased my mind considerably, it gave me time to consider the near- and long-term problems of using FOCOS.

My greatest concern was the body cast issue. We were a twelve-hour ride by bus or an hour by air, but how can a child sit or even board a bus or plane in a full body cast? The only way he could be transported would be in the back of the pickup truck. The obvious safety issues aside, I couldn't imagine half a day in the back of a truck, on the dusty roads with temperatures reaching 100 degrees. Even if we could find and afford a place in Accra for him to live while recuperating, he would need twenty-four-hour care. I could afford the time but would need at least one other person to make that idea work. Lastly, without a clear idea of how to ensure he would get the therapy and follow-up support needed, would it be fair to subject him to such extreme surgery?

Bill and I prayed on how to proceed and decided that FOCOS was not a viable solution. It was time to find out what His plan was for Saviour. We were drawn to Matthew 7:7, "Knock and the door shall be opened for you." This was the instruction from our Lord, so we decided to send one last request to our Shriners contact explaining the obstacles we were facing.

On March 14, I wrote to ask if I could arrange a meeting with the doctor to plead my case in person. I explained the visit to FOCOS Hospital and the evaluation and costs we were given. I explained that we were raising the money but had my concerns about the body cast and the logistics of getting him back to Sang. I also told them that there was minimal, if any, post-surgery rehabilitation available in Ghana. I told them that after a great deal of prayer, my heart told me that having the surgery and recovery here in South Carolina would result in the best outcome for Saviour. Bill and I were willing to commit the time and money necessary for Saviour to be in the US for as long as surgery and recovery would take. I hit the send button and we prayed and prayed.

On March 17, I received this message:

Dr. Westberry has agreed to see Saviour. Let me know next week what time frame you are looking at in bringing him to the US. He will need to remain here in the states with you for four months.

* * *

We were ecstatic! The doctor's change of heart eased so many concerns we had and eliminated all the hurdles having surgery in Ghana had imposed. Unfortunately, the hurdles cleared were replaced by the chief hurdle and red-tape maker of the world, the US government.

Before a surgery date at Shriners could be made, we had to know approximately when Saviour would be cleared to travel to us. My many experiences with air travel and Africa time aside, we were in unchartered waters when it came to getting a visa to come to the US. Getting my visa to go to Ghana consisted of filling out a form, writing a check, and sending my passport to the Ghanaian embassy in Washington, DC. A few weeks later, my passport was mailed back with the visa inside. The first time, the visa was invalid by the time I intended to travel but eventually, we got that fixed with a multiple visit visa being issued. But that was the Ghanaians; we are talking about the American embassy in Accra. This should be much easier.

We learned that Sister must apply for and be granted the passport and visa for Saviour before we arrange the flight. No surprise to us as a ten-year-old orphan usually doesn't come with a passport. So Sister Stan acquired one for him and then began what can only be described as the most torturous process I've ever witnessed. As you may remember from an earlier chapter, Sister would have to take Saviour to Accra each time the embassy required until the visa was issued. In Saviour's case, this was a total of three trips at a cost of $1,200.00 or to put it in perspective, a month of meals at Nazareth Home for God's Children.

As part of the visa application, we were instructed to get a letter from the surgeon at Shriners describing the reason for bringing the child to the US to receive surgical care and treatment. Trip one to the Consular Section ended with the first rejection because the letter from Shriners was addressed to William and Joan Tucker and the US Embassy. The clerk said it needed to be addressed to the Directress of the Nazareth Home for God's Children, and the salutation should read Dear Sr./US Embassy Ghana.

The people at Shriners were understanding and we were able to resend the appropriate letter a few days later. Further scrutiny by the clerk and a scrupulous adherence to minutia resulted in a second rejection and meant another email to Shriners requesting a third version of their letter because "the letter from Shriners did not include contact phone numbers and email address for the doctor." It was also suggested that the letter state that Shriners Hospital has a history of donating care to international children in need and that you are willing to treat Saviour for his disability from cerebral palsy.

Rejection three by the clerk (which does rhyme with jerk) was because there was not enough medical information provided. Apparently having a crippled child sitting right in front of you is not sufficient proof of their needing medical help. We decided to get the doctor from FOCOS Hospital, as well as the pediatric doctor from Tamale Teaching Hospital, to write notes as they have both examined Saviour. This should cover everything they could possibly want, right?

Don't ever underestimate the power of a bureaucrat. This time Shriners needed to include a dollar amount that the hospital was willing to spend on the child! It wasn't enough to say that no expense would be incurred by the family, orphanage, or the government; they wanted an exact amount! This surgeon is going to be tired of us before we even get to Greenville.

As the day for his appointment at Shriners drew closer, our anxiety grew. After calls to our state senator and inquiries to a friend at the State Department, we were told by State that "our system shows the visa was issued on 14 June" and that it might take several days for the passport, with visa to be delivered to the applicant. We prayed that "the system" knew what it was talking about as Sister Stan needed to fly to the US on June 18 to attend a fund raiser for the orphanage in Colorado. The plan was for her to bring Saviour to New York and for one of us to pick him up there and bring him to Charleston. I know what you're thinking, "our plan."

We had an appointment at Shriners Hospital for June 26 and everything seemed to be falling in place. On the appointed day, Sister headed to the Embassy to pick up Saviour's passport only to be told that the recently issued visas were at the DHL office to be delivered to the applicant. Back in the car to race across town to intercept the package except DHL had no record of the passport being delivered to them so it was back to the Embassy arriving just in time to find the doors locked for the weekend.

Imagine Sister's frustration. She was traveling with two hand-icapped children. One heading to Colorado with her for follow-up treatment and Saviour. She had to be in Denver by June 20 for the fundraiser and time was running out. Fortunately, she had family in Accra who agreed to give Saviour and Mr. Alhassan a place to stay over the weekend. Since Saviour would now have to travel alone, she made arrangements with Turkish Airlines to fly him as an unaccom-panied minor paying an extraordinary fee to do this. My concerns were not while he was flying but during any layovers. Who would be with him? He had only been on an airplane one or twice for the short trip from Tamale to Accra and had never on an international flight. I could only imagine how terrified he would be. On Monday, the passport and visa were obtained and Saviour was taken to the gate at Turkish Airlines. The attendants took one look at the ten-year-old whose legs were permanently curled up under him and immediately refused to let him board! Yet one more rejection for this poor child.

Bill and I were at a loss. I was willing to travel to Ghana to pick him up but my visa had expired, and it takes weeks to get one. Sister had made it to Colorado but asking her to immediately turn around and make a second trip for Saviour was out of the question. As it turned out, Colorado was the source of the solution to our problem. Another volunteer who made regular trips to the orphanage lived there and dear Mama Leelee agreed to make the grueling round trip for us. She would leave Denver for Accra on the next available flight.

Twenty-two hours later, she would arrive in Accra, pick up Saviour at the airport, and immediately return, bringing him directly to us in Charleston. God bless her. She left for Accra on June 22. The next day I received a call from Shriners, reminding me that Saviour had an appointment the following Monday. I told them we would be there, knowing that the Good Lord would forgive me my little white lie. I trusted that He was going to make it happen, He didn't bring us this far for nothing! My Mantra was "Jesus, I trust in you"

Lee and Saviour arrived in Charleston at 6 p.m. on Sunday June 25. We waited anxiously as the passenger filed through the security gate until finally, Lee appeared with Saviour, who was being wheeled around by an airport attendant. He was flashing that famous grin, partly at seeing me but mostly, I'm sure, because he knew his trip was over. We transferred him to what would be his main means of mobility for the next six months, a bright yellow children's wheelchair.

It was a short drive from the airport to our home, and we arrived there just in time for some dinner, his first bath in a bath tub and a good night's sleep before the car ride to Greenville in the morning. My husband remarked that, "Maybe God works on Africa time too." I was just glad that He had answered my prayers. As it turns out, He had more than a hectic plane ride in store for Saviour. On the flight, he was seated next to a gentleman from Holland who lived and worked in Atlanta. While Saviour did not speak, they would become good friends, and he asked if he and his wife could come see him after his surgery. But that's another story.

* * *

We got up early the next day, June 26, in order to make it to Shriners Hospital in Greenville, South Carolina, in time for our 12:30 p.m. appointment. As we drove along, Saviour would look out the window, not saying a word, just taking it all in. We had been told that he was probably autistic and did not speak. That turned out to be the misdiagnosis of the decade. Once Saviour gets to know you, he gets very chatty. His lack of early vocalization and Ghanaian accent makes him a little difficult to understand at times, but he is very verbal. We think the diagnosis was due to the fact that he was always crawling on the ground with the babies at the orphanage. With no one to talk to, there was no reason to talk.

The drive was thankfully uneventful and we were greeted by the admission staff with smiles and encouragement for Saviour, something this hospital never seems to lack. The rest of the day was filled with tests, including x-rays, a session with physical therapy for their evaluation of his abilities and limitations, and of course, an examination by the doctor. Thankfully, Saviour, unlike Abraham, was malaria-free and all his pre-op tests said he was ready to go.

It was during these tests that I found out our ten-year old was a little over three feet tall and weighed in at thirty-two pounds. By the end of the day, Shriners had planned out his operation and scheduled it for the following Wednesday. So it was back to the hotel for dinner and some much-needed rest.

Our day off was mostly an effort to relax and introduce Saviour to some of the many blessings and wonders our nation has to offer. Given the limitations of his childhood to date, everything was new and wonderous. On the advice of a friend, who is a doctor that does some missionary work, we got Saviour a pair of sunglasses, not for the sun but because the bright colors of the trees and grass and other things we took for granted that could overload his senses. We put a few miles on his wheelchair, visiting the animals at the Greenville Zoo. He loves animals, dogs in particular, and has often expressed the desire to "work with animals" when he grows up.

In another first, he got to enjoy a uniquely American culinary delight, the corndog. We both slept well that night which was a blessing in that it prepared us for a few rocky days that followed.

The morning of his surgery had finally arrived. The staff at the hospital again did everything they could to help us relax. He got to pick out the design on the casts he would have on his legs after surgery and was then wheeled into a special room the children, who are having surgery, get to visit. Its walls were lined with all kinds of stuffed bears donated by Build a Bear, and the children get to choose any one they want to take home.

Saviour would choose the Soldier bear dressed in a camouflage uniform, just like the colors of the cast he'd chosen. He would earn a total in three Build a Bears in the years to come. Then it was off to prepare for surgery. He was a little groggy as they wheeled him out to the operating room so I was the only one who was truly anxious as he disappeared through the double doors.

Surgery seemed to take forever, but I'm sure that is a unanimous feeling among parents. Over the next few hours, Doctor Westberry and his team performed a number of procedures that I will share in some detail to give you a feeling of the enormity of the surgery and an appreciation of the strength and courage Saviour has. I did not know it at the time, but before beginning the operation, Dr. Westberry and his staff always pray over their patient, asking God to guide them and keep the child safe from harm.

As I sat in the waiting area, Saviour would undergo first a right femoral and tibial rotational osteotomy. Translation: they would surgically fracture his right femur and right tibia, turn it, and keep it in place with plates and screws. Next both legs would need surgery to lengthen the medial hamstring. This surgery is recommended for very tight muscle tone known as spasticity, which causes a child's hamstring muscles behind the knee to become overly tight. Without this, a child may have to walk in a crouch because the legs won't straighten.

The last procedure was a gastrocnemius soleus recession, again in both legs. The calf is made up of two muscles, the gastrocnemius and soleus muscles. The gastrocnemius is the larger muscle. It has two separate heads that attach the thighbone (femur) to the heel (calcaneus). The gastrocnemius and soleus join at the base of the heel to form the Achilles tendon. The gastrocnemius allows the knees and feet to flex and it powers the ability to push off the foot. When the muscle is tight, the ankle's movement becomes restricted, causing excessive force on the foot and ankle. The recession releases some of this tightness.

* * *

Saviour's bed was wheeled back to his room with his skinny little legs casted from above the knee to the end of his toes. They were split down the center to allow for any swelling that might occur and to allow monitoring for bleeding. He looked so small and helpless lying there. The doctor told us that everything went as expected. He would have the casts reinforced before he was discharged and would then need to return on a weekly basis to gradually stretch the casting at his knees to slowly straighten them out. At four weeks, the cast would be removed so a molding of his legs could be taken. These would be used to build a solid ankle foot orthotic which would help him stand. He would then be re-casted for another two weeks, after which he would get his final fitting of his orthotics and begin physical and occupational therapy.

When Saviour woke from his surgery, he was in a great deal of pain, as expected. What wasn't expected was his reaction to the narcotics they would give him for the pain. They first administered them through his IV but this almost immediately triggered a severe bout of vomiting. Tried as they did, the nurses and doctors could do little to manage his pain without him throwing up. The rest of the day and all of Thursday were extremely rough for the little guy, and I felt guilty that I had not prepared him emotionally for how he would feel immediately after surgery. We had only discussed how the doctor would help him to stand and maybe even one day, walk.

The gentleman Saviour met on the flight came with his wife to visit him. They brought him some gifts, and we took some pictures of them by his bedside. It wasn't the best of visits as he was having a rough time of it but Mr. John and Ms. Lynn took it in stride and have come to visit him several times since. It was fortunate we took those pictures as, to this day, Saviour has no memory of them coming to the hospital so I guess the pain medicine had some effect.

Saviour was discharge on Friday, just two days after his surgery. Given his level of discomfort and inability to keep pain medication down, I did not foresee an easy trip home. They tried giving him some pain medicine just before we headed out to the elevators to go home. Saviour returned it to them before we even got on the elevator, so it was back to the room to clean him up and take a few emesis bags with us for when he got sick on the ride home.

The normal four-hour ride home took closer to five, as we kept stopping to readjust the pillows under his legs or use the urinal as he needed to get rid of all the IV-fluids they had given him. Difficult as this trip was, I kept thinking how impossible the journey in the back of a pickup truck would have been in Ghana. The entire time on the road, I never heard a complaint from him. It was the first of many times his courage, patience, and determination to succeed would both inspire and humble us.

Now that we were home, we tried to establish some sort of routine for Saviour that might help him cope with his world turned upside down. Fortunately, our home was a single-story ranch so getting him around was easy. As the drugs wore off and the pain receded, the days became a source of constant wonder for Saviour.

He had his own room, a first in his life. I actually believe he was a little lonely, and fortunately, the room had two beds so I was able to stay with him the first week or two in case he needed help at night. We also had pets in the house; two dogs, Bear and Zoe, and a cat, Ishtar. Saviour was used to dogs, chickens, pigs, and even cows wandering through the compound and the chickens would sometimes sneak into a room, looking for a place to nest but having pets in your house was not the Ghanaian way. Dogs were outside and scavenged for food, being tolerated only because the served as a kind of alarm if strangers tried to enter the compound. Our three pets would be a great source of companionship for him and his natural love of animals shone through as they all accepted him immediately as a member of the pack.

Visitors were a great source of relief from the monotony of sitting in a chair all day with your legs sticking out in front of you. Sister Stan took a detour on the way home from Denver to check on her little one and her cousin. Father Timothy joined us, adding a special prayer over Saviour for a speedy recovery. Sister remained with us for several days, and we took the opportunity to venture out a little and get ourselves used to traveling with a child in a wheelchair.

One trip was to visit the Fire Museum in North Charleston. He was fascinated with the big trucks and other equipment on display and laughed when Sister got behind the wheel of an antique fire truck and pretended to be driving to a fire. His day was made when he got a fireman's hat to take with him and you can just guess what one of his costumes would be for Halloween. Sister left to visit some parishes in New York as part of her "begging tour" to help fund the orphanage, and then would return to Ghana.

I think Saviour's favorite time though, was when our granddaughters would come to visit. They would stop by to introduce him to new things such as balloon fights, arts, and crafts and the latest rage, making *slime*! The four of them became quite proficient in making this stuff, and we found ourselves ordering gallons of glue and a lot of food coloring just to keep up. Fortunately for us, the girls took their creations home with them. I'm sure their parents will forgive us for that, someday.

* * *

During one of their joyous welcomes. Saviour is on the ground to my right and Abraham is by my shoulder

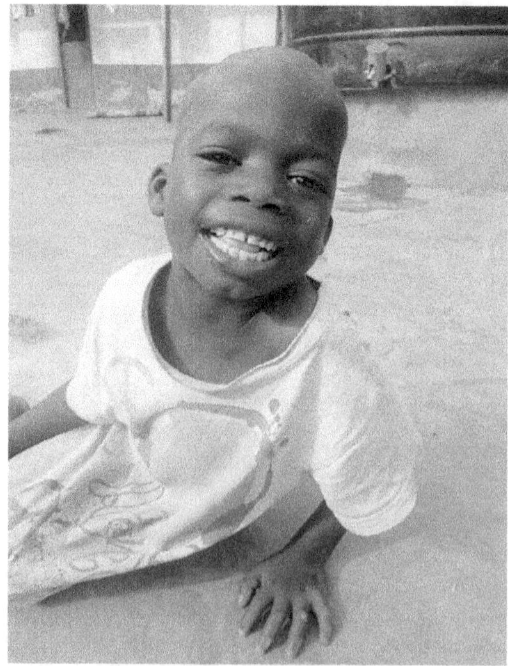

Saviour at around 4-5 years old. Always smiling

With Nicholas helping him get around

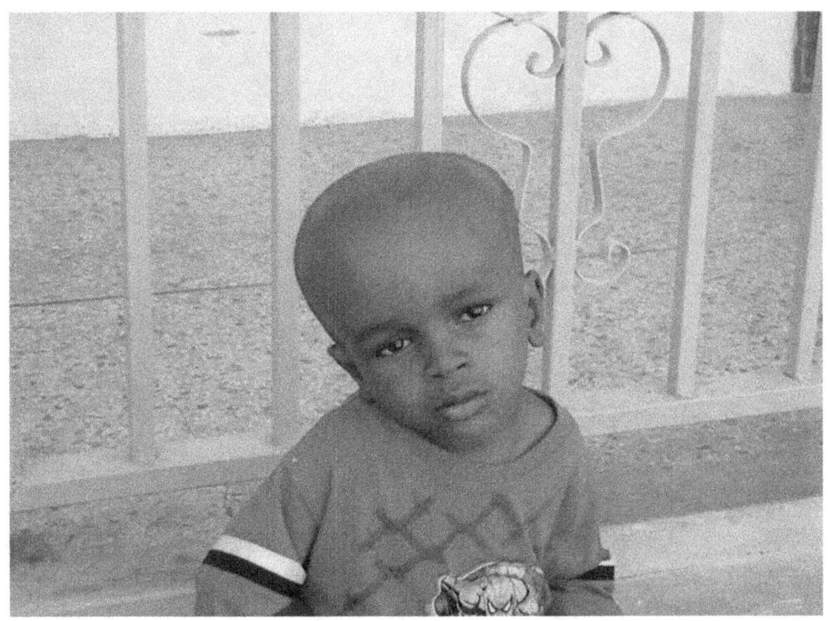

Abraham before his surgery

The playground arrived just before I left

This is much better than playing with empty boxes

Dressed up for Mass with Eva (now Sister Maria Goretti)

Little Anna's final resting place.

Just arrived in the U.S. for the first time (age 10)

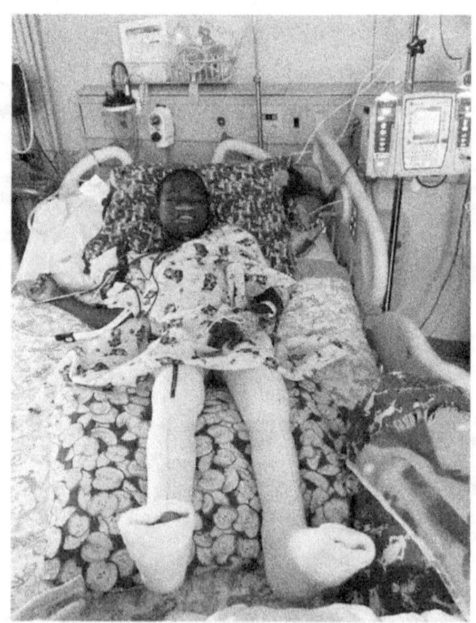

Days later, coming out of his first surgery.
He would need a total of six over the next few years

Sister Stan visiting Saviour with our granddaughters
showing him how to make "slime"

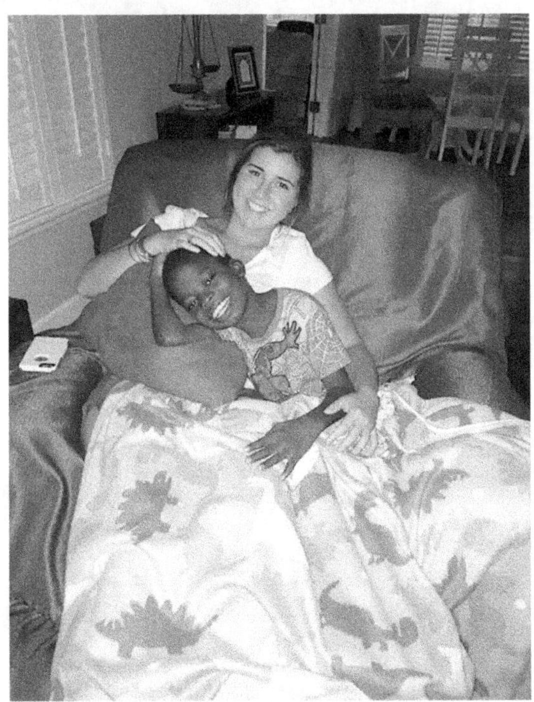

Resting and recovering with Miss Amanda

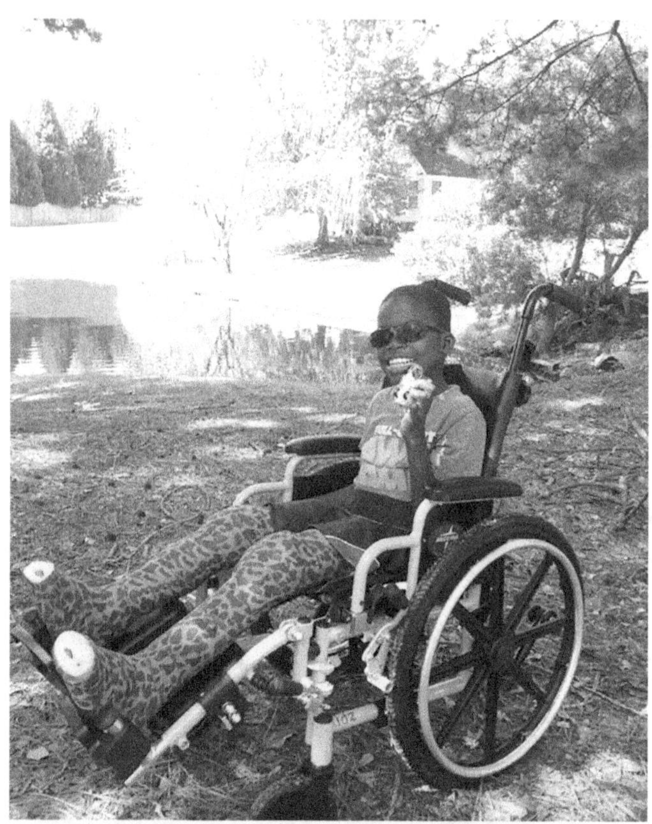

Post-op daily neighborhood "walk" with Mr. Bill

Sometimes a granddaughter would help out.

"Reading" a book at Shriners. It would be three years
before he would begin to read on his own.

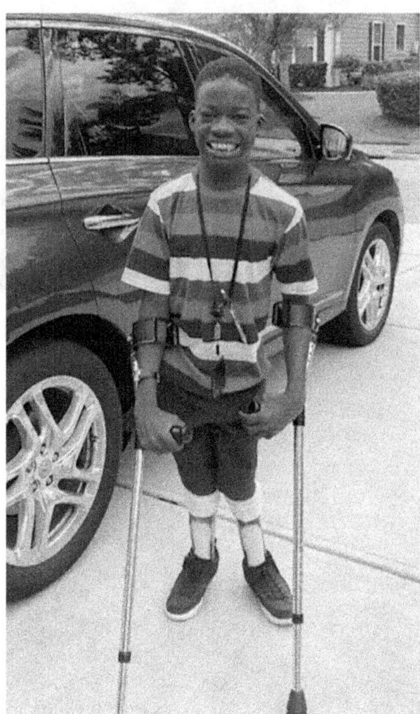

Coming home from school. He walks very
slowly but always with that smile

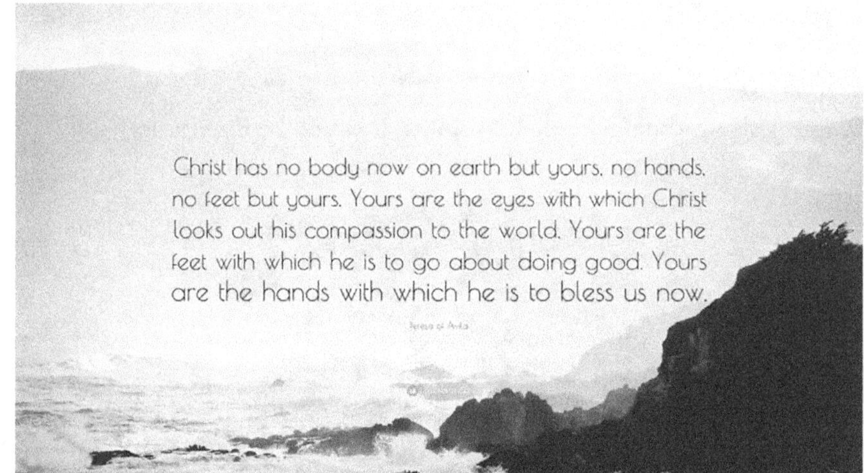

St. Theresa's words that got me on that first airplane to Ghana

Finally, the day arrived when his casts would come off for good. Rather than just the day trip we were used to, this time we would be there a whole week. He was fitted with his first leg braces called Ankle Foot Orthosis or AFOs. This is a leg brace that runs from below the knee to the tip of the toes in order to control the position and motion of the ankle. Then there would be a week of intense physical and occupational therapy for him. Thankfully, Shriners provided a room for us at the hospital for this time, so keeping up with the schedule they had was relatively easy.

We drove to Greenville and, after settling into our room, headed downstairs for the big reveal. I couldn't wait to see Saviour's straight legs and his reaction to sitting normally for the first time in his life. As they cut the casts off, I could see the scars from the surgery but they meant nothing to wonderful sight of his skinny little legs sticking straight out in front of him. Saviour's beaming smile quickly faded though and tears ran down his face as he tried to tell us he was paining. This is the children's way of saying they hurt. Fortunately, the nurse quickly realized the problem and told us that, after so much time being immobilized in the casts, his leg muscles were probably in spasm. We were able to comfort him and they massaged his legs until the "jumping," as he put it, went away.

Shriners has weekly meetings to introduce the staff to the children that are on the schedule for the following week. They also show pictures of the children and give them a little history of the child and their journey so far. Saviour was an instant celebrity and his story of survival and determination to stand and walk spread far and wide.

A woman from Shriners public relations department approached me and asked if we could do an interview with a local TV station. Everyone at Shriners had been so generous with their time and talents in helping Saviour, I found it impossible to say no even though I was no spokesperson and very uncomfortable getting in front of a camera, let alone being interviewed. This feeling doubled when I learned that two TV stations wanted to cover his story. All I could do was pray the good Lord would give me the words as He had with Hallie on the radio.

The only word I can think of to describe Saviour's therapy is grueling. His day would usually start with an hour or so of physical therapy (PT) followed by another hour plus of occupational therapy (OT). After a break for lunch, it was back to the center for more PT, a review of his treatment and sometimes, the introduction of a new exercise or piece of equipment they had made to help him. I was tired just from watching as they stretched and pulled at his legs, had him try to stand up from a sitting position or stand him between two balance beams and try to have him walk.

I've discussed Saviour's desire to walk and neglected one other problem caused by his CP that would greatly impact his ability to become independent: his right hand. From the first time I saw him, Saviour's right hand had been clenched in a ball with his thumb folded under and sticking between his middle and ring fingers. Anything he had to do, had to be done left-handed. The OT specialist was extremely patient with Saviour and commented on how tightly he held his hand closed. Over the next few days, she would gradually get him to loosen up. We would often hear him talking to his hand telling it to "open" whenever he had a new task to try. Eventually, his hand loosened up enough that they were able to get a splint on it to keep his hand open, hoping the stretching of the muscles would eventually help him gain some use of the hand.

Through all the poking and pulling, standing and stressing, Saviour would keep that smile going, flashing even bigger when a challenge was overcome or a therapist would praise his efforts. His mantra was "never give up" and it worked not just for him but for us. During Saviour's final session, his therapist was showing us what we could do to help him continue to grow stronger. She also mentioned she had a friend at the Medical University of South Carolina (MUSC) in Charleston who might be able to help. Little did we know at that time what an incredible blessing this would be.

* * *

Our week at Shriners had opened many doors for Saviour and for us. One we never expected was when a young nurse approached me and said she and her husband would like to look into the possibility of adopting him. This was unchartered territory for me, and I quickly reached out to the Director of Sister Stan's Children to see what, if any chance, there was for him to be adopted.

Sister Stan's Children is a 501(c)3 set up to help support sister in her efforts to fund the orphanage. Its board is made up of all volunteers who have been to Ghana and seen the challenges. They work constantly to make sure the children have what they need. I thought this request might be met with some resistance as Sister's vision was to keep the children in Ghana as an example to the natives that spirit children are not evil and possibly break the grip of old customs and superstitions that had damaged or killed so many children in the past.

It was finally decided that the only person who could answer my questions was Sister, so when we got home, I placed the call. Phone calls to Ghana, especially to Sister Stan who is constantly on the go, are hit and miss. Oh, they have cell phones all over Ghana; cell service is another question. I finally did get through to her and, after some prayer and thought, she agreed we should explore the possibility of adoption.

In the coming months, when we would travel to Shriners for a checkup, we would stay with Melissa and her husband, Robert, so that they could get to know Saviour better. This was a true Godsend for us. Instead of six or seven hours in the car plus the time at the hospital filling our day, we could break up the trip into two days making it much more bearable for us. Saviour was now getting a little more confidence and quickly became comfortable with this new arrangement. For him the big attraction was Dolly, their dog. Given the chance, Dolly would lick Saviour's face stopping only on the third or fourth command to do so while Saviour would laugh and laugh. While our dogs loved to be petted, they were not lickers, so Saviour would have to wait for a trip to Greenville to get his doggie bath.

These trips also gave the Smiths a chance to get to know Saviour outside the hospital arena and, while they had grown children of their own, they still needed some adjustment to handle Saviour and his needs. Melissa's first lesson was on bath night. After getting

Saviour settled in the bathtub, she proceeded to turn on the shower for him to begin his bath. Saviour was used to the cool bucket baths at the orphanage but was completely unprepared for the rush of cold water that hit him. Melissa said, "He didn't jump too much but his eyes nearly popped out of his head." Saviour still jumps a little when then shower comes on but we all learned to get it a little bit warmer before turning it on him.

The Smith's came up with other ingenious methods for taking care of him. Concerned that he might need someone in the middle of the night, they asked him to call out as loud as he could. For Saviour, this was a medium stage whisper. So Robert rigged up a cow bell over his bunk bed so all he had to do was pull on the cord to get our attention. I never heard him use the cowbell at night, but he sure enjoyed practicing in the evening before bedtime.

Saviour was also fascinated by another new friend he met at their home, Alexa. Robert had wired the entire house and could manage all of the lights and television from anywhere in their home. As wonderous as this was for Saviour, the real magic was when you got Alexa to play a song for you. The song craze at the time was Baby Shark and Saviour would start to giggle as soon as it started playing.

The really interesting thing is, the little "autistic child who did not speak" spent hours trying to get Alexa to listen to him. Now Alexa had grown up with American accents at the Smith's house. Saviour's impeded speech, combined with his African/British accent, posed a whole new challenge for her. It took some time but eventually Alexa learned "Alexa, play Baby Shark!" in "Saviourese," and we would be regaled with its playing over and over again. Without planning it, we had found some electronic speech therapy for him. Robert and Melinda would present Saviour with his own Alexa that Christmas, and she continues to help him with his speech. Thankfully, Baby Shark is no longer top of the charts.

* * *

The rest of Saviour's stay with us that first time was filled with all kinds of wonders for him. He got to experience celebrating the

4 of July, not his holiday but when in Rome. He liked the food and the neighbors next door came over to watch the little fireworks display, courtesy of Mr. Bill. The performance got mixed reviews with plusses of the pretty lights and colors, a minus for the loud noise, and a definite thumbs down for the embers drifting down. We're not sure where his fear of fire and getting burned comes from, but it remains with him to this day.

At first, while he was in leg casts, his days consisted of being wheeled around the neighborhood by Mr. Bill, watching cartoons on the TV, and trying out new foods at dinner. While getting to meet neighbors and watching the Canadian geese, squirrels, and egrets play around the ponds was okay, we all couldn't wait for his cast to come off. Thanks to an introduction from Shriners, we got to meet with a doctor at MUSC who not only heads the physical therapy department there but volunteers her spare time to helping children like Saviour when she is not overseas, helping them in their own homes.

I don't know where she gets the time and energy, but I thank God for her when I see Saviour overcome another hurdle in his therapy. If she was not working with Saviour on a new exercise, she was arranging for us to borrow equipment to use at home or getting us a special tricycle on loan for him. She even worked on a toy electric car conversion for him, which proved semi-successful though Bill still has tread marks on his shoes from trying to help him steer.

Saviour would receive occupational therapy at MUSC, helping him to straighten out and start limited use of his right hand. As expected, he quickly won the minds and hearts of all the therapists there and would be invited to come to a class of OT students. Dressed up as his favorite character from TV, he was escorted around the classroom, showing off abilities and limitations and doing exercises to help him improve. The teacher made him the boss of the class, selecting students to help him and encouraging him to try new things.

On the way home, he announced that today was a "great day," a phrase he would use over and over in the coming weeks. Throughout the rest of his stay, we were constantly blessed with people willing to share their time and talents to help him.

We had a swimming pool and thought it would be great therapy for him after his casts came off in early August. Summer in Charleston is filled with good days to swim and we had a lot of fun helping him float and trying to move his legs up and down to swim. We later found out he wasn't afraid of the water but was surprised as he thought to pool was filled with drinking water. No Northern Ghanaian would ever consider wasting such a precious commodity for play. But he did like splashing around and really enjoyed our pool parties when the granddaughters would come and Mr. Bill and Mr. Craig would have cannon ball competitions.

It was during this time we were trying to work on the basics of his education. At the age of ten, Saviour could chant his ABCs and count to ten. This was the sum total of the education offered at what passed for a school in Sang village. Everything was verbal as there were no school supplies for actually writing the alphabet or doing simple addition and subtraction. Sister has since made an effort to identify the children who are educable and find sponsors to send them to a proper school in the city. Saviour, however, was unable to identify numbers, letters, or colors.

We had a friend of the orphanage, Amanda, come to visit Saviour from Halifax. She was studying to get her teaching degree and would spend hours reading to him and even made some learning tools to help him identify colors and numbers. After she left, we attempted to carry on with his education but neither of us had any formal training, and it had been over twenty years since we'd had to try and help our girls with their lessons so we were at best, rusty.

I think going over the colors was the most difficult thing for us. No matter how often we went over red, yellow, green, blue, and orange, everything we pointed to was orange to him on his first guess. This would have been okay with us if we were Clemson fans but our daughter and son-in-law were University of South Carolina graduates! We became frustrated at times until our daughter mentioned that his brain was busy learning to walk for the first time in his life, and it probably took up all of his concentration and focus. Once he didn't need to concentrate on moving his muscles, he would be able to start learning. She was so right!

* * *

This chapter in Saviour's life would not be complete if I did not take this time to thank a young Canadian student and her mother for their time, talents, and compassion for Saviour during his recovery. We did not know Amanda and Candace before they came to visit, but we could tell that Amanda had a history with Saviour, and I'd like to let her tell you in her own words how this little boy with a big smile came into her life. Here is her story.

I first met Saviour in 2016 when I went to Ghana for my developmental studies degree through Saint Francis Xavier University. My Ghanaian professor saw my passion for working with children and arranged my placement at the Nazareth Home for God's Children. Sister Stan welcomed me into her home to live for four weeks. During this time, I had the opportunity to meet and get to know the most amazing and beautiful children. Little did I know that one boy would change my whole life forever and become someone who I hold so closely in my heart.

Saviour and I have been through a lot together. I was drawn to him right away. His smile was full of love and his eyes were so bright with hope. At first, Saviour wouldn't say much to me, so we had to find our own way of communicating. He would smile for yes and not smile for no (at least try not to smile).

During my first week there, I noticed something was off with Saviour. He wasn't feeling well, and I couldn't figure out what was wrong. I tried getting the staffs' attention, but I didn't want to push too hard being new at the sanctuary and all. As the days went on, Saviour kept looking worse and worse. I noticed his knee had grown three sizes bigger than normal. When I asked the nurse at the sanctuary, she informed me that Saviour couldn't walk and always pulled himself around so he probably just bruised his knee. I knew this was different because he started running a temperature, and that's when I went to Sister Stan.

Sister Stan told me I could take him to the Sang clinic the next day. In the morning, I gathered Saviour up in his wheel chair (which was missing a couple parts and didn't work very well.) It was my only way to get him to the clinic, so off we went. As we walked down the Sang Road, many people would yell in confusion, asking what I was doing with that little boy. When we finally reached the Sang Medical Center, I handed them Saviour's health card, and we waited.

When we got into the doctor's office, the man looked at Saviour's knee and said he had to get rid of the fluid buildup in his knee, a procedure that, in Ghana, did not get any anesthesia. I held Saviour down on the medical bed, looked into his eyes, and kept telling him everything was okay as the doctor cut open his knee and drained the fluid. I always knew Saviour was strong and a born fighter but, in that moment, this little boy cried and screamed in my arms, and I promised him and myself that I would stand by him for the rest of his life, so that he would never again have to fight alone. After the worst part was over, the doctor informed me that Saviour also had malaria. I spent the next couple weeks nursing Saviour back to health.

Saviour and I were joined at the hip after my first week. We would hangout often at the sanctuary. He really enjoyed coming down to my room with some of his friends to look at comic books and eat chocolate puffs. Saviour showed me the ropes at the sanctuary, and I spent each day getting to know him and the others. Saying goodbye to Saviour and the other children at Nazareth Home for Gods' Children was one of the hardest things I've ever had to do. I was always told about heart break, but I never truly understood how it felt until I said goodbye to Saviour and the other children.

When I came home from Ghana, I couldn't get Saviour out of my mind. Sister Stan put me in contact with a nurse who did work with Nazareth Home for Gods' Children named Joan who I now call Momma Joan. Momma Joan and her husband, Mr. Bill, fought for Saviour and blessed me with the opportunity to continue my relationship with him. The second time I saw Saviour was in South Carolina in 2017. Momma Joan and Mr. Bill welcomed my mother and I into their home, without knowing anything about me except for my relationship with Saviour. Visiting Saviour during his rehabilitation was one of the greatest moments of my life. I am forever thankful for being able to introduce

Saviour to my mom, Candas. I know he changed her life just as he did mine. He often does that to everyone he meets.

My friendship with Saviour grew stronger and stronger. We spent every day together. We worked on colors, sounds and numbers, but I knew he was so determined to walk that his physical health needed to be his focus before he focused on his studies. We swam in the pool, played Mexican Train, watched movies, went for bike rides, and had a Ghanaian night. Saviour would love watching videos on my computer of the children in Ghana, and he would think they were on Facetime. One of my favorite memories with Saviour is lying in his bed, reading stories, and laughing until we fell asleep. When I said goodbye to Saviour, I promised him the next time I would see him would be back at his home in Ghana.

In 2019, I surprised him at Nazareth home for Gods Children where I was able to meet up with Mr. Bill before he took Saviour back to South Carolina for another surgery. Since then, we have been able to FaceTime and see how much he has grown both physically and emotionally. I feel so grateful for being a part of his life and can't wait to see what he does next. Whatever it is, I know he will give it all his energy and, along with that smile, he will succeed.

* * *

Mr. Craig, Aunty Jody, and the girls were a great source of entertainment and education for Saviour that first summer. We took trips with them to the aquarium where, for the first time, Saviour saw a fish that wasn't sitting on a plate waiting to be eaten. He loved the huge tanks with thousands of fish swimming around but wasn't too keen on feeding the sting rays. They would take him to the beach where he would not only see more water all at once than he had ever seen on his life, but it moved and made noise.

Our granddaughters showed him the fine art of sand castle building and would help him hunt for sea shells and other wonders to be found at the beach. They rented a beautiful cabin in the mountains where he was introduced to his first real forest, a train ride through the mountainside and, at the bonfire that evening, Smores.

He would have so much to tell his brothers and sisters back at the orphanage, I'm sure he'll never be considered nonverbal again.

Bill and I tried our best to listen to what God had to tell us but we were never certain that He was always listening to us. Saviour would give us an incredible confirmation that He does listen. On August 21, Charleston, South Carolina, would be one of the prime viewing locations for a total eclipse of the sun. Not witnessed here since 1918, there was a big media buildup for the event, and parties were planned to enjoy what was probable going to be a once in a life time experience. Saviour was going to get the science lesson of his life, and we were going to have a party!

We invited the neighborhood over for a BBQ and pool party. I found a documentary on TV to show Saviour how the moon obscures the intensely bright light of the sun, allowing the much lighter solar corona to be visible. We were in the zone of totality, with the eclipse peaking around noon. What could be more perfect?

As the time approached, Saviour grew more and more agitated and insisted he be taken inside repeating over and over again, "I do not want to see!" What I never factored in was that, in his culture, a solar eclipse was attributed to supernatural causes or regarded as a bad omen. He was very frightened that the sun would not return and that would be the end of us. He would tell us later that he asked God to take the eclipse away.

As we were taking him inside, ominous clouds began to gather overhead. By the time the eclipse began, we had a small window between several large, back clouds to view the first sliver of the moon's shadow appearing over the Sun. In a matter of moments, the clouds completely block our view and rain began to fall, a little at first but soon, it was coming down in buckets. We all raced inside to join Saviour, making it just in time for the heavens to open up and the rain to begin falling like it would never stop. Stop it did eventually and the clouds broke up just as the eclipse ended. Mr. Craig, Jody, and Co (the family as Saviour put it) lived about twenty miles from us and had a beautiful view of the entire eclipse. Our once in a life time experience would have to be viewed on the local news report that night and in the pictures our family and friends took nearby.

They say when a child speaks, God listens. This would not be the last time Saviour would prove that he had the ear of God the Father.

* * *

Although we hadn't planned it, Saviour was going to experience three more holidays celebrated American style before he would have to go home; Halloween, Thanksgiving, and Christmas. They say Halloween has international origins but that doesn't include Ghana and definitely does not include the near gluttonous consumption of candy. We, of course, wanted him to have the full experience so there he was on Oct 31, dressed up like his favorite cartoon character with no idea about what would happen next.

Our dentist, who loves the business Halloween drums up, had been treating Saviour without charge and, as usual, he was the darling of the office staff. We were asked to bring him by, and they all gushed over him and his fancy costume. Then the big moment, he got his first piece of candy. His "Thank you, may God bless you" further endeared him to the staff, and they all waved goodbye as we walked out of the office. One of the staff at the office across the hall had seen this all and rushed out with her bowl of candy for him to select from. I was as shocked as her when he said, "No thank you. I have plenty." Tried as I might to explain to him, the idea of all this candy being just for him was too much. All night long, as we walked through the neighborhood with Jody and Co, I would remind him that he could take a piece and say "Thank you" or "Happy Halloween." I think we still have some of the candy he got that night in the back of the freezer.

We also had the opportunity to take him to watch the Charleston Battery play soccer. Football is played everywhere in Ghana. No nets needed, just a ball and children! We arrived before the gates opened and the little boy in the yellow wheelchair drew smiles from everyone else in line. A policeman stopped and talked to him and asked if it was okay to take a picture. Saviour was enjoying the attention but little did we know how much he would get.

We shared his story with a man at the ticket counter, and he mentioned that we should have called the front office beforehand, and they would have made special plans for him. Next thing we knew, he came to us and requested that Saviour be taken in his wheelchair onto the field. It seems the Battery had a Ghanaian player the year before and the players wanted to welcome Saviour! Bill took him out and the coach let him hold the game ball while they waited for the players to appear. As the team came out on the field, they all stopped to say hello and give him a high five along with some words of encouragement. He was grinning from ear to ear and will forever be a big fan of the Black and Yellow.

Every day was an adventure for Saviour thanks to the caring and sharing of family and friends. In early October, he had his first boat ride where he saw dolphins up close, got to "swim" in the river and even found a special rock that still sits on his dresser to this day.

Our granddaughter had her birthday party at the local ice-skating rink and invited Saviour to attend. We weren't sure how much fun it would be for him to sit in the bleachers and watch the other children skate around, but he wanted to go. We were so happy when the rink owner gave us permission to put his wheelchair onto the ice. Bill strapped on some skates and pushed him around until a new friend, a young man named Timmy, asked if he could take over. Bill had played ice hockey before but that was many years ago and his legs weren't what they used to be. Timmy was the exact opposite and he and Saviour raced around the rink, swerving around slower skaters (like Bill) and making quick stops to create a shower of snow. Needless to say, he loved it!

* * *

Our last trip to Shiners was supposed to be for a routine checkup before Saviour would return to Ghana. It turned out to be a little more than we expected. By this time, he was just being introduced to crutches. The original expectation was that straightening his legs would make it possible for him to sit properly in a wheelchair and the crutches were considered a long shot but I think the doctor sensed his drive and determination. As we waited in the exam room, Bill commented that it might be a big surprise for the doctor if Saviour walked over to him using his crutches. Without hesitating, Saviour stood up and slowly walked to Doctor Westberry when he entered the room. We could see the surprise and delight in the doctor's eyes as he examined Saviour. He then asked is we could wait while he checked on something.

We were unaware at the time that Shriners has a tradition known as "Randy's Celebration Bell." It is a brass bell that hangs in the main lobby. This bell is usually rung by patients that have turned twenty-one years old and have aged out of their care. The hospital staff assembles and cheers on the patient as they move on to the next phase of their life. It's a touching ceremony and the goodbyes are heartfelt and moving to witness. What we didn't know was that the bell was also used to acknowledge major milestones or successes of a patient.

We headed downstairs and were greeted by Doctor Westberry who explained that Saviour's progress was completely unexpected and proved how determined he was to walk. As the staff assembled, we moved over by the bell and waited. On signal, Saviour walked oh so slowly the last few steps by himself, grabbed the cord, and gave it a tug. At the first little peal from the bell, the whole staff exploded in cheers and whistles, handclapping and shouts of encouragement. I don't know who was more surprised or moved, Saviour or Bill and I.

According to the terms of Saviour's visa, he had to leave the country every six months and wait twenty-four hours before he could return. Knowing this, we planned to return him to the orphanage shortly after the first of January. Our hopes were to get him a multiple visit visa now that we knew his potential was unlimited.

We set up a follow up appointment for September 2018 with the expectation that the plates and screws in his legs could then be removed, and he would get a new pair of AFOs as he grew. We topped off our visit with a special ride in Robert's Mustang for ice cream. When Robert took the top-down on convertible, you would have thought Saviour was back in the cold shower his eyes got so big.

The next day we said our goodbyes to the Smiths; made easier knowing we would see them again next year.

* * *

As Christmas drew near, we experienced an unusual event for Charleston, snow flurries. This lasted just long enough to dust the chairs around the pool and disappeared within minutes of the sun breaking through the clouds. It did wake up old memories of growing up in Pennsylvania which we shared with Saviour, telling him it was too bad we didn't have time to take him someplace where he could experience a real snowstorm. We should have kept our mouths shut. Saviour said he wanted to see real snow and that he would take care of it. After our experience with the solar eclipse, I should have called the local weatherman to warn him.

We woke up on January 3, to heavy overcast and a light rain falling, and I thought it would be a quiet day inside playing games and watching TV. A good chance to rest before the long trip to Accra in a few days. The rain switched to freezing rain, but we weren't too concerned. We had plenty of groceries and would need to restock in a day or two. By noon, the freezing rain had changed to snow, and now it had our attention.

The local news broke in with weather updates that we could not believe. The local weatherman started his update telling us that "Charleston sees snow about once every five years and measurable accumulation about once every ten years, so this event is very rare." By the end of the snowfall, we had an official 5.3 inches of snow on top of the layer of frozen rain, the third largest snowfall in recorded history for Charleston!

I know my family members who still live up north will never understand this but Charleston was in full lockdown for the next four or five days. There are about as many snow-removal trucks here as there are palm trees in Alaska. This meant that the roads quicky became narrow avenues of rutted snow and ice, nearly impossible to navigate. The sun would come out at times, melt a little snow only to have it refreeze as solid ice. Charleson airport had absolutely no snow removal equipment and would remain shut down for the next four days. Our flight was in three.

Bill got up very early the morning of our planned departure to check the news. Charleston airport remained closed for at least twenty-four hours. The decision was made to try to drive to Atlanta to pick up what would have been our connecting flight. The roads were still very icy and rutted and the inexperienced drivers made navigating out of our neighborhood extremely difficult. If it was like this all the way, we'd never make it to Atlanta in time. We were about ten miles from the interstate, and it was white knuckles all the way but, thankfully, the main highway was clear and we made it to Hartsfield International Airport with enough time for a quick kiss goodbye. After a hurried run to check in and get past security, we made our boarding time with minutes to spare. It was not until we were in the air that it dawned on me how God had been in charge the whole time.

Because of the flight changes needed to get Saviour to us, he had flown through Atlanta instead of the usual route through JFK in New York. His return flight mirrored his original route so, for the first time, we were scheduled to fly Charleston to Hartsfield not Charleston to JFK. While the drive to Atlanta was difficult, a drive to New York would have been impossible. I imagine God thought, "Hey, Saviour wants to see some snow; why not! I can do that get him home safely too."

* * *

Surprisingly, the drive to Atlanta was the hardest part of the trip. After meeting up with Marie, the physical therapist, and now my regular travel companion, we arrived in Accra. As we stood in line to have our passports and visas checked, Saviour began silently crying. I thought it would be difficult for him to adjust back to life in the orphanage after six months in the United States with all the new experiences and friends he had there. I asked him if he was alright, and through the tears, he stuttered out, "I miss Mr. Bill!" I tried to explain that he would be coming back in the future, and we could FaceTime Mr. Bill when we got to the orphanage.

For all the delicious foods, trips to the mountains, ice skating, to the aquarium and beach, he missed my husband. Bill had been a big part of Saviour's rehab, carrying him around or taking him on long walks in his wheelchair. He was also the chef in the family and had introduced Saviour to many new foods and other experiences like making a snowman.

Saviour not only was walking for the first time in his life, he also met his first father. Having been abandoned at the age of three, he had few memories of family life and, try as she might, Sister Stan could not provide the intangibles a true family provides for her orphans. By now, Nazareth Home for God's Children had grown to over forty orphans and, while providing safe housing, regular meals, and loving attention to all of them; she could never compete with the one-on-one experience he had had while with us in Charleston. There were one or two men who help her at the orphanage but rarely did they have time to interact with the children and almost never individually with a child.

Our arrival at the orphanage was greeting with the typical song of welcome and rows of smiling children. They were all amazed to see Saviour walking and loved his bright yellow wheel chair. I whispered in his ear, "Everyone is so happy to see you." But the emotions, along with the exhaustion of the trip, were too much and the tears returned.

The next day, after a good night's sleep, his beautiful smile returned. With the help of Mr. Prince, a relative of Sister Stan who visited once in a while, Saviour enjoyed "kicking the football" with his friends for the first time. This was always his dream. He was still far from running and playing like the other children, but he totally enjoyed this momentous first step.

Unfortunately, the orphanage had continued to grow in our absence. There were at least a dozen new children including James and Phillip, abandoned because they had extra digits on their hands, and a tiny baby who weighed in at just over two pounds. Sister named her Kelly after another nurse who had come to help the children. As time drew near for me to leave, I tried a video call with Mr. Bill that went quite well, partly because he was adjusting and also because we told him that we would be back to pick him up in six or seven months for follow up surgery at Shriners. Imagine being exciting at the prospect of having surgery.

I'm sure it seemed like forever to Saviour, but I was back to pick him up that September. While the visit was short, I was able to see how much Abraham had improved since his surgery. He had grown to the point that he could hold his head straight and the smile on his face made everything we'd been thought together worth it. Unfortunately, things had not gone as well for Saviour. The demands of caring for over sixty children with minimal staff support meant luxuries like taking time to strap on Saviour braces and giving him physical therapy gave way to bathing him, placing him in his wheel chair, and having the children fight over who could push him around all day. It was so frustrating to see his potential and yet know that the things he needed to succeed did not exist in Sang village or anywhere in Northern Ghana.

The trip to Shriners for checkup and hardware removal was pretty routine. The doctor was pleased with his healing but the lack of regular physical therapy in Ghana had limited his recovery. New braces or Ankle/Foot Orthotics (AFO's) and crutches would help him while he was with us. His determination to improve was also a big factor. Unfortunately, the visit also brought some bad news from Melissa and Robert. Melissa had developed a serious health issue and after a great deal of prayer and soul searching, they had decided that adoption was no longer possible. We were as heartbroken as they were but understood that her health had to come first and are grateful that they have chosen to stay in contact with Saviour. We always get together when we visit Shriners, and he enjoys hearing about the adventures of their dog, Dolly.

* * *

We made a post operative trip to Delaware to visit my family. I am the oldest of ten children so meeting my family can be a little overwhelming but he took it in stride. He particularly loved spending time with my grandnieces and nephews who were close to his age. Watching him interact with them made me think that, while being here was a definite plus for his medical health, having to spend his days with two old people couldn't be his idea of a good time. If only we could find a place for him to have regular interaction with his peers. God would finally give us the answer to this but not just yet.

Saviour would stay just three months this time but still got to enjoy Halloween (Superman this year) and even got to take six weeks of therapeutic horseback riding lessons. As with all animals, he loved the horses, and the teachers loved him. They even arranged for a local television station to come out and do a story on him and his horse-riding skills. He was becoming quite the ambassador for Sister Stan.

Another opportunity we had missed on this trip, was a week long, intensive occupational therapy clinic offered at The Medical University of South Carolina call "Hand to Hand Camp." This was a clinic, given by the students that would inhibit the use of his good hand with a puppet, while playing games with him, forcing him to use his impaired hand. We weren't sure how successful this would be for him as his right hand was a perpetual clenched fist, but the idea was exciting, and we were told he would be more than welcomed next year if he got here in time. I wasn't sure if it would be financially responsible to fly him here for a weeks-long camp but, you guessed it, God had his plan.

At our last checkup at Shriners, Doctor Westbury proposed another procedure for Saviour to help straighten out his legs and foot even more. He was still severely knock-kneed and tended to roll his left foot inward as he walked. The procedure, called guided growth, involved inserting plates and screws into the growth plates of his legs to stimulate and guide the growth outward to correct the knock-knee. Saviour was coming to the age where a growth spurt could be expected and the doctor wanted to do the surgery within the next six months. The other stipulation was that the procedure required him to be checked regularly for eighteen months to monitor his growth and determine when to remove the growth plates lest he become bow legged. Plan noted, Lord.

* * *

As Amanda mentioned earlier, Mr. Bill would make the trip to Ghana in May of 2019 to surprise Saviour and bring him back for his next surgery. While the flight from Charleston to Accra was uneventful, getting to Tamale proved the usual challenge. After five hours of waiting for the flight to be called, he was informed that all flights had been canceled, and he should go back to the counter to book a new flight. Bill has traveled a lot overseas and was semi-prepared for what was to follow. In Ghana, the concept of forming a line or queue has not taken hold. After an hour or so of elbowing his way through a disorganized clump of unhappy passengers, he had his new reservation and was saved by Mr. Emma who had thoughtfully booked him into a hotel nearby for the night.

The next day proved far more successful and Bill arrived at the orphanage during siesta, so he decided to settle into his room and surprise Saviour after the rosary that afternoon. A friend of Nazareth Home had donated the funds to have an outdoor grotto dedicated to the Blessed Mother built outside the main building. This is where the sisters, novices, and most of the children gather every afternoon to pray the rosary.

Bill was fully expecting the children to be a bit distracted but was not prepared for the cow wandering through the grotto or for it to deposit a smelly gift between the rows of benches. One of the novices very nonchalantly reached behind her, grab a small shovel, walked over to the steamy pile and removed it all while leading the children in their recital of the Hail Mary.

As the service ended, Bill walked up behind Saviour who was sitting in a dilapidated wheelchair. He couldn't read Saviour's expression as he said hello but could tell things had not gone well for him the last few months. While the staff and children all did their best to help him, he had not been able to use his AFOs or do any real walking since returning. When you have seventy or eighty children to care for, fulfilling individual wants and needs is a luxury, especially when the needed medical facilities and specialists are non-existent.

Bill would spend two weeks there, watching the children play and getting firsthand experience with the joy of having a large jar of candy amongst a larger group of children. He walked with Sister Stan as she inspected the new dormitory she was building. The government had informed her that, since some of her children were growing older, boys and girls had to be housed in separate buildings, not just different wings of the same building. The expense of this was a new challenge for her but she had faith that the Lord would provide. She also showed him where the new housing for the novices and sisters would be and the foundation of what would be the chapel. These two projects were taking second place to the new dorm.

On the day of their departure, Sister brought the children out onto the front porch to pray for Saviour and Mr. Bill to have a safe journey and to say goodbye to Saviour as he left for his next adventure. Each child stepped forward to give Saviour a hug, saying goodbye and hoping he would return safely soon. Little did we know that this would be his last day at the orphanage for a long, long time.

* * *

By now we were very comfortable with the routine of getting Saviour to the US, preparing him for surgery, and getting him to and from Shriners for his procedures and follow-up visits. Our biggest challenge would be the government bureaucracy and the intransigence of the technocrats at the Department of Homeland Security, usually referred to as DHS but maybe more appropriately DUH! You'll understand shortly.

The operation was relatively minor by medical standards but would require twelve to eighteen months of monitoring to remove the hardware once the desired growth was achieved. Saviour's visa was still valid but, the six-month requirement to leave the country was problematic to say the least. Bill had spoken to a relative at the State Department about this and was told it would be best to contact Customs and Border Protection to get a definitive answer on how to handle the problem. Several calls to them resulted in finally talking to a human being who told him that DHS was the authority that needed to be contacted. It only took three tries to get a live voice on their phone only to be told that DHS usually takes its lead on matters like this from, you guessed it, the State Department.

After a lot of independent research, Bill finally found the forms necessary to request an extension of stay for a B1 visa holder. All this entailed was several reams of paperwork, affidavits from the Doctor and hospital, reassurance that we would be financially responsible for Saviour and all his needs for the duration of his stay and, of course, a $450.00 filling fee. The package went off in August with many prayers and not a lot of confidence in ever getting the requested extension in time.

Meanwhile, Saviour recovered from his surgery quickly and was enjoying his time back in America. He had left Ghana before Sister could get him his second vaccination against Hepatitis-B so I made arrangements to take him the South Carolina Department of Health and Environmental Control. They were the most affordable option for his inoculation. It was a longer drive as we had sold our home and moved to Mount Pleasant to be closer to the grandchildren. What a life changing visit this turned out to be.

The woman at the clinic was going over our paperwork and I lamented that, with all this time he would be spending in the US, we didn't know what to do to keep him entertained or how we could afford sending him to a school. The woman gave me such a look and told me he had a right to an education and that going to a public school would not violate our promise to provide for all of his needs. What a blessing her advice turned out to be.

I contacted the Charleston County School System and asked if it would be possible to enroll Saviour in a special needs class. We were asked to come down to the main office for an interview the following week. Bill, Saviour, and I arrived a few minutes early and were greeted by a counselor who took us to an interview room. Imagine our surprise when we sat down to a large table around which were seated a counselor, two special education professionals, a physical therapist, occupational therapist, and a speech therapist.

After explaining our situation and the fact that Saviour had never been in a real school before, they worked up a plan to enroll him in the sixth grade of a local school nearby. We were a little leery of the mainstream approach but they told us that at thirteen, he could not be placed in the first grade and work his way up. He would have special education classes intermingled with two or three mainstream courses each semester and would have a teacher's assistant with him at all times. Our only responsibility was to help him at home with his studies and get him to and from school each day.

Saviour's first day at school was almost anticlimactic. We were concerned that his educational delay would make him a target for ridicule by his peers and prayed that, as they got to know him, they would accept him into their world. He was moving around well and had been given a special walker by the therapist at Shriners that gave him a lot of independent mobility. Because of the weakness of his right hand, they had incorporated arm rests on the walker that gave him additional support as he pushed the walker forward. Saviour became very proficient with this walker and could navigate the hallways easily, helping him to feel more like the other students.

Mornings were Bill's shift so he would help him dress, get him breakfast, and pack his lunch, then drive him to school. A teaching assistant would meet them in the parking lot and escort him to his homeroom and to each class, bringing him to the pickup line in the afternoon for us to take him home. On the ride home, it was pretty obvious that he absolutely loved school. All he could talk about was his "new friends." The children were extremely kind and reached out to him whenever they felt he needed some help or just a high five. The teachers quickly fell in love with him and within a week, he was on the school news broadcast as the student of the week. God had answered our prayers a hundredfold. School was such a positive experience for him that he actually looked forward to Mondays and approached every Friday resolutely as he would have to spend two days with the old people.

* * *

While Bill and I had discussed our lack of experience with raising a young male, one thing we had not previously given any thought to was raising a teenager in the era of social media. We started when he turned twelve with an old but usable iPad. We loaded apps like ABC mouse that would help him with telling time, reading, and basic math. Once he started school, we began hearing about more interesting things his "friends" had on their computers like Minecraft, Roblox, and YouTube. We put parental locks on it, and he had to ask permission before downloading any apps or making any purchases. For a kid who could barely read, he sure could find any app that caught his fancy or item he wanted to purchase on Amazon. I believe that children today have special parts of their brain dedicated to interfacing with computers.

As I noted earlier, Saviour was a small child when he first started his trips to the US. He weighed only thirty-two pounds and was fairly easy to lift him into cars or his wheelchair, even with full-legged casts on. As time went on, he started to grow and grow and grow! Before we knew it, we had a teenager in our home, he had a growth spurt of almost two feet and sixty pounds. His voice was no longer the cute squeaky sound we had become familiar with but almost overnight became a very deep manly voice. All the signs of puberty were emerging quite rapidly. We started hearing about "my new friend at school named Peggy" quite frequently. His smile when he said her name made it obvious to us that he was experiencing his first crush.

One day after school, I noticed Saviour seemed a bit forlorn and not his normal smiling self. I asked him what was wrong and he said, "Today, Zhy asked Peggy for her phone number, and she gave it to him. Why would she do that?" I explained that teenagers carried cell phones and would get the numbers of their friends to send text messages and occasionally call to talk to them. Then he said, "I guess I won't have a phone until I'm sixteen or eighteen." I told him that he needed to learn to read and spell in order to use a cell phone. He then said "I think I'm jealous!" That was quite intuitive for him to say. It was also a signal that he was figuring out how to push our buttons to get what he wanted but, that's a big part of growing up so I didn't mind.

Bill and I discussed this after Saviour went to bed that night and we decided that since we were due to get new phones, we would give him one of our old ones. The hope was it would encourage him to read and spell. He was in a special education class for reading and math but was mainstreamed into social studies, history, world studies (where he met Peggie). He really loved these topics and learned so much. Reading was still a challenge but slowly, the light was flickering.

We presented the phone to him on a Friday, and he was ecstatic! We showed him some of the ways to use it and loaded our numbers for him. We helped him memorize his new number which he retained with incredible speed. He would use it in the morning to call and say he was ready to come down for the day. Monday after school he came home very excited. Peggy gave him her number; life was good once again!

I realized he was lacking basic socially skills, and we would need to start from the beginning with him. He was told that even though he had her number and could text her, he still needed to ask permission to call or FaceTime her. Thursday, he came home to announce that Peggy said he could FaceTime her over the weekend. I may be exaggerating but I think he went to bed extra early that night so the weekend would come sooner. Bill went up around eight o'clock the next morning and found out that Saviour had been up for some time and had FaceTimed her at 7:00 a.m.! The poor girl was so sweet she didn't get angry with him. I told him that most teenagers like to sleep in on the weekends, and girls especially don't like to be awakened and to be on camera before they comb their hair. Lesson one of many complete.

His infatuation with Peggy continued for a few months, and it was hard to get him understand that she liked him very much as a friend but not as a girlfriend. I knew he understood when his eyes teared up and he asked, "Why does love hurt so much?"

Friends from church who had sons suggested some books that explains how God created us to be male or female and how each matures into adults at different times and in different ways. It walked us through the emotional minefield known as "The Birds and Bees."

I answered his questions and told him we hoped he would develop into a godly man who would respect himself and others. He definitely has the emerging body of a man, but the knowledge of a child, and we pray that we will have the words to help him grow emotionally into the fine young man we know he wants to be.

* * *

The next part of Saviour's story is painful to remember and to tell. There was a second couple that voiced an interest in adopting Saviour. We arranged meetings between them, and they began spending more and more time with him. It seemed to be a perfect solution to his problem with the weekends. This couple had far more energy than us and the added bonus of owning five dogs! Not only was he much happier visiting his doggie friends, but Bill and I would get a much-needed break a few days a month.

Saviour was unaware of the legal aspects but really looked forward to seeing them and going to their home. As time went on while unraveling the red tape, it became obvious that their intention to adopt faced some major obstacles. Ghana followed The Hague Convention with regards to the adoption process. The estimated cost, according to the adoption agency, would be nearly $50,000.00 and included a requirement they spend two separate months in Ghana. The final blow was that they could not preselect the child. He or she would be chosen for them.

They made the painful decision to stop the process but insisted they still loved him and wanted to be a part of his life. We reluctantly agreed, and he would spend some weekends with them. They even agreed to keep him for almost an entire month when the schools were shut down because of COVID. Suddenly one Sunday, he was brought home by the husband, and we were told his wife was experiencing "female problems." That is the last time we had any contact with them. All text messages and phone calls were ignored. They just walked away from him without any explanation. Saviour continued to reach out by text and spoke of them often, wondering what he did wrong. Slowly over the next year, he quit trying. I told him I didn't know why they would not answer him. His response was, "She never said goodbye."

* * *

While a lot of negatives things can be linked to the COVID pandemic, it proved the catalyst to a major decision that would affect Saviour and us beyond anything we had ever imagined. I had just returned from a quick trip to Ghana when the first news stories about COVID began to appear. Bill and Saviour were planning a trip over in early May, after school let out as the extension on his visa ran out at the end of that month. The trip would allow him to see his old friends and reset the DHS clock for another six months. Everything was ready to go when overseas travel was shut down indefinitely.

While it wasn't quite time to panic, we were unsure about what would happen if we could not get Saviour out of the country in time. More importantly, we could not be sure Saviour would be allowed to return given the new travel restrictions. If he had to remain in Ghana, the guided growth procedure would have to be terminated before he left. On top of that, we knew from past experience that he could not get any physical or occupational therapy there. All of the doctor's efforts and Saviour's hard work would be for nothing. I prayed and prayed that God would provide an answer to this problem, and He really surprised me this time.

As you know, helping Saviour, Abraham, and all the children at Nazareth Home for God's Children was what I called my retirement vocation. My husband supported all of my efforts emotionally and financially and was always willing to chip in to help. He would fix wheelchairs, adjust crutches, and was our driver for many of the three-to-four-hour trips to Shriners. Being an early riser, he agreed to help Saviour with his morning routine but usually referred to himself as Saviour's equipment manager.

Bill had his own calling as a volunteer with a disaster relief organization that often had him away from home for a week or two at a time. I knew he needed that time to reconnect with military friends and share the comradery that only those who have been through the same hardships and experiences of being in a disaster zone affords. He would always come home tired but happy.

As the time approached for Bill to take Saviour back, I grew more and more apprehensive. What if Saviour was denied reentry? What if the growth plates in his legs weren't removed on time? Would we find him sitting in a wheelchair the next time we saw him or worse, crawling on the ground? I voiced a lot of the concerns to Bill and was taken completely by surprise when he came out and stated that we could not let all of Saviour's hard work be wasted and the only way to be sure of that was to keep him here for as long as necessary. I was overjoyed and apprehensive at the same time. Keeping him here would allow me to get him the treatments he needed and afford him the opportunity to go to school and realize his fullest potential. It would also mean that two retired seventy-year-olds would be responsible for raising a teenaged boy, something neither of us had ever done.

* * *

Bill put together another packet (and check) to request a second extension citing the travel restrictions and Saviour's age and medical needs. We knew that as long as the application was under consideration, he would be considered legal, but it quickly became apparent that this was only a short-term solution. While looking for an alternative solution, Bill happened to mention our situation to an old high school friend. She gave him the name of a friend who just happened to be an immigration lawyer with instructions to contact her if he didn't satisfy our needs.

Bill called and found out that there was an alternative to adoption that could be worked out for about one tenth of the cost. Bill and I would need to petition the court for legal guardianship of Saviour with the reason for the request being that he was an abandoned child. We could then apply for a green card for Saviour under these special circumstances. The idea seemed perfect except that we would have to ask Sister Stan, his legal guardian in Ghana, to admit he is abandoned to support our petition.

Sister loves all of her children dearly, and I knew signing such a document would cause great spiritual and emotional pain. I was even more apprehensive when the lawyer sent the petition to us to forward for Sister's signature. Legal terminology is quite blunt and cold, and we knew that Sister, rightly so, would take the wording personally. It was never her intention to put any of her children up for adoption. She loves every child and plans to keep and love them for as long as they are in need. For the majority of them, that means the rest of their life. Sister is devoted to showing the community these children are not evil spirits and, by their example, end the superstitions that have led to the death of so many innocents.

We were so relieved and grateful to Sister Stan when she decided to place Saviour's needs above her desires and signed the petition in our favor. Our first court hearing was virtual thanks to COVID, and we expected the decision to be pretty straight forward in our favor given that all parties agreed. The judge had other plans though and ruled that, without better documentation, proving Sister Stan had legal custody of Saviour, he could not determine if she had the authority to sign that custody over to us.

His greatest concern was that he did not want to make a ruling only to have Saviour's parents come forward at a later date to contest. He decided that a guardian ad litem needed to review the case, contact Sister and the Ghanaian authorities, and present her findings to the court at a future date. He set the maximum fee the Guardian could charge at $3,000.00 with a retainer of $1,500.00 at the time they are assigned.

After everything else, I must admit this was just a bump in the road to us that we knew God would take care of in His time. We contacted the lawyer assigned as the guardian and she agreed to take our retainer and begin her research. We explained that documentation in Northern Ghana was not what she was accustomed to seeing and responses to written requests would be answered in Ghana time. She understood, started her research, and set up a time to come visit our home and talk to Saviour. During her visit, we filled her in on Saviour's history and Sister Stan's devotion to the children. She said she would call Sister with a few questions and hopefully, have her report ready in short time. Our next hearing was set for July, just a few months away.

The day of the hearing arrived, and we prayed that the guardian had been able to get everything she needed to make her recommendation to the judge. Sitting in front of our computer, waiting for the session to begin, we could only pray that today would be the day. Our lawyer, the guardian ad litem, and the judge all came on line and we quickly realized our prayers had been answered. The judge stated that given the documentation presented and with the wholehearted recommendation of the guardian ad litem, he would grant our petition. It was like a great weight had been lifted off us and we could not thank them all enough.

We received one last blessing when the judge asked if any of the officers involved had any last comments. The guardian ad litem stated that she had been really impressed with Saviour and our determination to help him. She told us that she would not only waive all fees for this case but would be returning her retainer. The judge could only say that this was probably the first case he had where a lawyer returned their fee to the client.

With that hurdle out of the way, we called the immigration lawyer with the good news. He said they could now move on the application for his green card once we provided him with the $1,200.00 needed in government filing fees. I could only think of how this would be no problem since we were getting our retainer back. The Lord does giveth and the government doth taketh away.

We are now officially Saviour's guardians, or Mom and Dad as he likes to say. His status allows him to get a green card and will greatly simplify keeping him here for the foreseeable future. We have petitioned the government to issue him a work permit, social security number, interim travel papers, and the green card. Almost a year later, we have the first two. The last two, we've been told, should only take another year or two. We pray they don't mean in Ghana time.

* * *

So far, I have told you a lot about what we have done for Sister Stan and specifically for Saviour. I'd like to spend a little time telling you what they have done for us. I have mentioned how my first trip to Ghana was a little unnerving because of all of the unknowns I was facing. Meeting Sister Stan and the children changed the direction of my life on a course that was both frightening and fulfilling. Sister has always firmly believed that if the Lord wants you to follow a certain path, He will always help you navigate through it. This is the belief that led her to leave the relative comfort of being a school teacher in Nigeria to sole guardian and mother to what is now over one hundred special needs children.

Even with the restrictions of COVID travel greatly impacting her ability to raise funds for the orphanage, she remains firm in her belief that God will provide. And He has been generous as we have learned that not only has sister finished the convent and chapel for her growing MASEL community but also has built a real school for the children living in the area.

Saviour has been an inspiration to both of us in word and action. From the start, he has always had a determination and willingness to attempt whatever we asked of him. His motto has always been "never give up," and it has carried him so far in such a relatively short time. Everyone he meets falls in love with his smile and are inspired by his strength and his eagerness to dare to be great. Mind you, his smile is sometimes a mask to cover fears. Given his early life experiences, we are amazed that he does not suffer from PTSD, but in truth, his greatest fear is being abandoned again.

Early on, Saviour initiated a morning custom that I so wish we had had with our children. Every school day, Saviour is dressed by 7:00 a.m. when Bill goes up to put on his braces and shoes. Bill would always have him stand up to make sure everything was fitting properly. One morning, Saviour stepped forward and gave him a big hug and said, "Thank you, Dad." What a way to start your day! This has become part of their routine, and Bill will admit he misses his hug when he's away or on the weekends when Saviour doesn't need help getting ready.

Saviour could often bring a totally new perspective to a situation, sometimes with brutal honesty. Asked by a teacher if any student could tell the difference between appetite and hunger, his response was "Hunger is when you don't have anything to eat for three days, and you think you're going to die." Another time he was asked what he liked about school in the United States. He told them his two favorite things where, here the teachers showed up every day and he didn't have to sit on the floor during lessons.

He has also made it possible for us to meet so many incredibly kind and generous people that have had an enormous impact on his life and ours. The physical and occupational therapists, as well as the orthopedic specialist who make his leg orthotics and have volunteered their time and talents to help him. The dentist who refuses payment for his checkups or any work that he needed done on that great smile. The friends and neighbors who helped fund his trip to a special therapy camp and always give him a smile and high five whenever they see him. The Boy Scout who worked to build a special walker that will give Saviour better mobility and the complete strangers who have walked up and given him a hundred dollars to, "buy something nice" (this has happened not once, but twice.) All of you have been such a blessing to this little boy, now a young man thanks to all you have done for him.

But probably the most important lesson he is teaching us is how wonderful life is no matter how mundane it might seem to be and that the people you meet every day are important. If Saviour sees someone at school or while we are out shopping and they smile at him or wave, they are his friend for life. He may not know their name, where they live, what religion they profess, or how they vote but he knows they are his friend. Not a day goes by that he doesn't announce, "Today I met a new friend." I wish I could say the same.

So this is Saviour's story—so far. Next year he will start high school and together we will face a whole new set of challenges and opportunities. High schools tend to be much bigger and where teenagers are concerned, friends may be hard to find. He will face a whole new set of social and educational challenges that we pray will not be too overwhelming for him. Then there is the not too small matter of his physical therapy, occupational therapy, and the prospect of one more major surgical procedure. We are making plans to help him and be there for him every step of the way but given how my planning has gone so far, maybe it would be best to just say that, as far as his future is concerned, God only knows.

ABOUT THE AUTHOR

J. B. Tucker is the pen name chosen by Joan and Bill Tucker to highlight their collaborative effort in writing this story. It also eliminated the need to play rock, paper, scissors to see whose name comes first.

Joan is a retired registered nurse, the inspiration for the story and the only reason you will understand the medical terminology in this book. She is also the source of many of the details about living and traveling in Africa and all the adventures one can face. Had she not listened to that first calling to "do more" for Sister Stan than write a check, this book would never have been written.

Bill is a retired government employee with over thirty years of experience including eight years active duty in the US Army and twenty plus years with the Navy and Department of Defense. None of which prepared him for dealing with the various bureaucracies both here and abroad but did teach him there is always a way around a regulation.

Joan and Bill would like to emphasize that this truly was a collaborative effort, much like their marriage. They had good writing days and bad ones. Memories shared and some forgotten by one but vividly remembered by the other. The third author, the Holy Spirit, made the whole thing possible. They hope you enjoy it.